MW01094336

A Distant CONNECTION

Letters From Prisoners Concerned About Today's Youth

KENNETH JAMAL LIGHTY

Order this book online at www.trafford.com
or email orders@trafford.com

Most Trafford titles are also available at major online book retailers.

Printed in the United States of America.

ISBN: 978-1-4669-9215-3 (sc)
ISBN: 978-1-4669-9217-7 (hc)
ISBN: 978-1-4669-9216-0 (e)

Library of Congress Control Number: 2013908119

Trafford rev. 08/07/2013

www.trafford.com

North America & international
toll-free: 1 888 232 4444 (USA & Canada)
fax: 812 355 4082

"Umuntu ngumuntu ngabantu."
(Zulu proverb)
"A person is a person through other people."

Acknowledgements

To my creator: I'm still trying to do the right thing, even though I fall short sometimes. I guess I will always be a work in progress in that regard. Don't let them pay more attention to me as opposed to the message that I hope to convey.

To my grandparents: Grandma, you're my rock, simple as that. I'm always at a loss for words whenever I think of you. I hope that I continue to make you proud, I'm doing the best that I can. Rick, you know you're my pops, I appreciate you for weathering the storms that I have created over the years. I love you both.

To my sisters: Toni, Lord knows you mean the world to me. They have you to thank because without your endless love, support, and commitment to holding me accountable, there would be nothing for them to read. I love you to death, no matter who doesn't. Keisha, mommy is surely smiling down now that we are back together. I promise not to let go. I love you.

To every single man that participated in this project at my request: You all are priceless. I have learned so much from you over the course of putting this together. It took much longer than I expected, but I never gave up because I knew that we had a serious message to give to the next generation. I hope that I exceeded you expectations. If you are a friend of a friend, that contributed some wise words, thank you. If I can help any of you in any way, let me know!

Peace

Contents

Preface

I wish that I could start this book off by telling you that I am an accomplished author, with a host of accolades and a trophy case packed with honorary literary awards, but I can't. To do so would damage the relationship that I hope to build with you over the course of reading this book, before it is even established.

The fact is, I am just someone who was once part of the problem, now trying to offer his help in finding a solution. I never set out to be a writer, I didn't attend college, and I never graduated high school. To top it all off, every word that you have read thus far, and hopefully will continue to read, was written in prison where I currently reside. I am simply a young man who has managed to better myself through a little bit of reading, and a whole lot of living. I firmly believe that these two credentials are the only ones needed in order for me to achieve the goal that I have set for this book.

My goal for this book is to speak directly to, as well as for, today's youth. It is my direct aim to provide some clarity as to why an overwhelming amount of our young brothers and sisters are currently entertaining, and for some, currently trapped inside of, a life of crime. There are two sources of inspiration that serve as the collective impetus behind this goal, both of which I managed to stumble upon by pure happenstance.

The first source came in the form of a television special that I found myself watching late one night while channel-surfing in my cell. Now I have to admit, I spent the first five minutes or so laughing to myself because what the television network had characterized as a "special", turned out to be nothing more than a heated (and often closed-minded) debate between young, inner city kids, and a panel of "successful" African Americans labeled as "Leaders". It didn't take long to see that both sides were so hell-bent on getting their points across to the other, that the art of listening had been omitted from the dialogue altogether.

Unbeknownst to myself at the time, I too had fallen victim to the same accusations that I had initially found myself hurling at the television screen, inadvertently rendering myself into a hypocrite. It wasn't until I stopped laughing, and started listening myself, that I managed to see part of the problem. Upon a closer look, I saw an overwhelming unwillingness, on both parts, to approach the discussion void of the pre-conceived notions that each side had been indoctrinated with in an attempt to establish effective dialogue.

This very obstinacy, has long attributed to the growth in the gap between the people that have been tagged as "Black Leaders", and those who have been written off as "troubled" or "lost", thus hindering the process of communication.

Through years of introspection and several botched relationships of my own, I have come to realize that to do such a thing is nothing more than a recipe for disaster from the start, no matter what your intentions are. The fact is, it is difficult to establish an effective bond or connection when you approach a situation, or in this case a person, with an already distorted point of view. You have to be willing to step into that dreaded gray area, that place of objectivity that allows you to effectively listen and analyze the topic in question, if you really want to understand the mindstate of an individual. So often people choose to lie to themselves, as well as other people, when faced with the difficult question: "What would you do?". It also helps when two people share a common denominator, such as a situational connection or a shared calamity, helping to avoid the feeling of being judged that often causes one to shut down and cut off communication immediately. Both empathy, and similarities in viewpoints and circumstances are important when trying to put the cause, as well as the effect, into the proper perspective in order to come up with a positive solution.

Today young people are exposed to everything under the sun, whether we as big homies, brothers, sisters, aunts, uncles, or parents, like it or not. Almost all of them can turn on the television and see whatever they may desire, but what about the overwhelming number of kids who are forced to take it one step further? What about those who day in and day out see murders and drug deals being committed on the way to school, or in front of their homes? What about those who choose to stay out as much as possible because they would rather hear gunshots and have the occasional fight in the streets than smell the foul stench of crack cocaine and watch those that they love slowly kill themselves? What about those who truly believe that you are defined by what you wear or drive, or how much money you can show at any given moment?

For these kids, there doesn't appear to be an off switch like there is on a television. Each day that they witness these things, they sink deeper and deeper into the deep ditch of hopelessness. These sad and unfortunate experiences soon start to trigger what is known as the "Domino Effect" because irrational perceptions start to form, which influences thought, which in turn influences behavior (which is the focal point for highlighting amongst young people by the media). This, is where it gets dangerous because the media has a tendency to bypass the cause and inflate the effect, creating a dangerous breeding ground for judgement and hatred between those who, if organized properly, could otherwise co-exist while simultaneously working towards bettering their common conditions. Now you have the very people who are supposed to be loving those who are "troubled", and doing what they can to understand and help, hating them and expecting nothing less than what is being perpetuated on television whenever they come in contact with them in their day to day lives. Negative expectations, mixed with perceptions shaped by hopelessness, are two of the main things that qualify young people for disaster and encourage them to try the street lifestyle.

Though I am now much older than when I was originally one of the young minds that I hope to reach, the fact still remains that I was one of them. This fact, as well as my obvious conditions of confinement, will help me to establish a connection with each reader as I share my thoughts and experiences in an attempt to pull back the curtains on a lot of false notions. Hopefully you will see that the experiences that you have endured, and the decisions that you have made, are not exclusive to just you. You share the plight of countless people not only in your city or town, but around the globe. We, like you, started to entertain, and eventually act on, thoughts of diving into the street lifestyle and all that came with it. This is what gives us all the credibility needed to share what has been learned throughout that journey, in an effort to spare you some of the bumps and bruises (if you're lucky). Through the words that you will read, if you are willing to drop your pre-conceived notions for a moment, you will find that the lifestyle that appears to be glamorous and fun, that was initially viewed as a way out, is nothing but an illusion, a gateway to a world that is far more dangerous and painful than the one that you wish to escape from. I won't sit here and lie in an attempt to get you to believe that some of it wasn't fun, but I can guarantee that in the end, the amount of happy days will not measure up to the amount of sad ones.

In the midst of all that came with the way that I was living, I, like you, had numerous people that I couldn't identify with telling me what I should do and what I should expect in the end. I shared the same ideology that I saw and heard those kids express that night on that television special when it came to positive advice from my elders and loved ones: "That's what they're supposed to say. As family, they're obligated to love me and care about my future. Times have changed anyway, they don't know what it's like, how they gonna tell me something?" It is at this very moment that I am reminded of something that an old timer whom I respect a great deal once told me years ago: "Youngin' I may have robbed some of the same places that you have years ago. The only difference is that y'all hold guns different these days."

Which brings me to my second source of inspiration, and the overall blueprint for this book. Shortly after seeing that special, it managed to stay lodged somewhere in my mind, even though I thought that I had long since moved on. About a year or so later, I came across a book that had piqued my interest for some reason. The book was titled: *"What Keeps Me Standing"* by Dennis Kimbro. It was comprised of a compilation of letters from black grandmothers who had been called upon to share their wisdom and advice to their grandchildren, and the next generation in general. The author had put out a mass e-mail inviting any and everyone to participate, and received a tremendous response. To my surprise, it turned out to be one of the best books that I've read to date.

Shortly after reading that book, I had an idea one night as I was doing my daily pace in my cell. I went back as far as I could in retrospect, and realized that not one of the street dudes that I had idolized coming up, either family or friend, had ever encouraged me not to chase this lifestyle. Now I am not blaming anyone, because we were all lost in the moments that we believed that we were creating, but I found it interesting nonetheless when I started to wonder if it would have made a difference. I also realized that I had never saw a book that was aimed at the youth in the streets in an effort to curve their interests to more positive things where the advice was coming from the very dudes that were being idolized, or rather represented what was being idolized, the street game.

Not being one to sit on a thought for too long, and seeing this thought keep manifesting in my day to day life, I decided to do something about it. I bought several books of stamps, and sat down to write letters to a diverse group of solid, well respected men, all whom I have met and managed to establish good relationships with throughout my journey in the prison system. In each letter, I explained my goal, and asked a single question: "If you could sit down and write a letter to one of today's youth, who is aspiring to follow in the footsteps of the lifestyle that you lived, what would you say?"

Now believe me when I tell you, I have love for, and am loved by a lot of individuals, but even I was somewhat shocked by the response that I received. I don't mean shocked at the fact that they wrote back, but rather by the way that they had all completely stripped away the masks that had ensured their emotional survival for so long. The altruistic nature in which they chronicled some of the tragedies in their lives, and exposed their shortcomings to whoever could possibly learn something from their past mistakes, truly moved me. As I prepared letter after letter, determining which ones I would use for this project and which ones would come in the follow up, I managed to learn new things about a lot of them myself, things that never found their way into some of our own conversations. It really re-enforced something that I had found myself beginning to question at one point, something that I once believed to be a fact: No matter how tough things may be for one man, the real ones always want to see the next one do better.

In the pages to follow, you will find letters from some of the most beautiful brothers that I have ever managed to cross paths with, both white and black alike. Brothers that have been tagged with the label of "convict" by a society that never really understood their pain. Instead they bunched us all in together and tried to write us off as "lost", like they are currently trying to do many of you, firmly believing that we were, and still are, the mindless animals that they so long ago locked away. I have tried my best to put together a variety, ensuring that all walks of life are addressed during this journey, minimizing in the least, eradicating at best, any possible excuses that a reader may try to produce in his or her moment of denial. There are letters from young men, older men, ex as well as current gang members, men convicted of drug-dealing, robberies, kidnappings, and killings, all from various states in the country. Whatever facet of the game interests you, believe that there is a representative in here with some sound advice and words of wisdom for you. There is absolutely no room for: "He doesn't know how it is!". These individuals have seen it all and done it all, and are here to reveal some of the hidden aspects of the street game that you usually don't stop to process until it is too late. They will also stress the importance of some things, as well as the futility in others, in an effort to lend some additional credibility to the advice of those that you love who would like to see you do better. I will also fulfill what I believe to be my obligation, as stressed to me by some of the very men that you will hear from, and share my thoughts and lessons with you in an attempt to inspire you to dare to do different.

Make no mistake about it, none of the individuals in this book, including myself, are perfect. We all still have mountains to climb in our quest to constantly evolve. There are days where we are peaceful one day, and raging the next, as we continue to fight the demons of our lower selves. The common denominator that is shared here is that we all care what happens to you. That, is what I hope that each reader will feel while reading this book. It's not about trying to scare you into doing things the right way, it's about a group of men who have not only been where you are mentally, but they also reside where you will end up physically if things don't change. I have no doubts that everyone will be able to relate to someone in here, and hopefully that will spark some change.

Be Inspired!
K.L

From: Kenneth Lighty
Washington D.C./Maryland

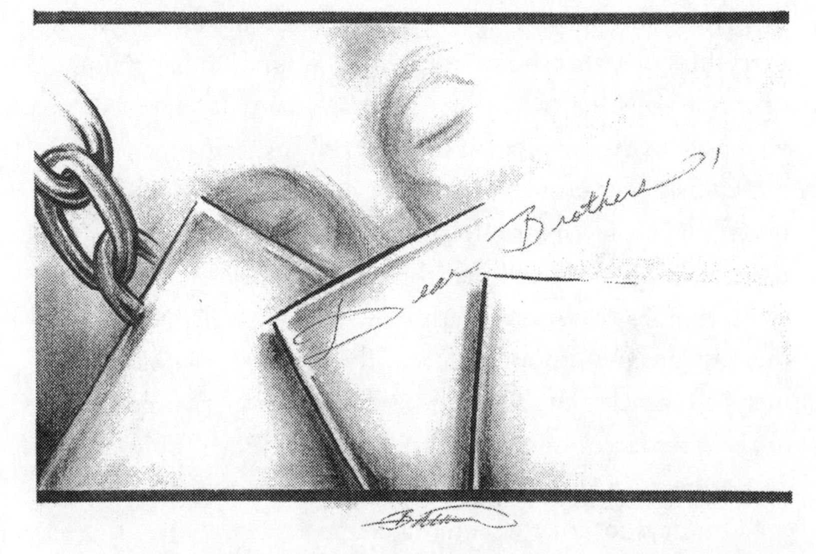

As I sit here in an effort to share some things about my life that hopefully will connect me with one of you, I am somewhat fearful of revisiting some of the places where my demons were conceived.

My father was murdered shortly before my birth, due largely in part to his active participation in the very lifestyle that I would eventually come to live as a young man. Like so many of us, he never imagined that he would see the day where he would become a victim of his own desires.

Obviously my mother bore the brunt of the heartache from losing my dad on many levels. She had lost the love of her life, forcing her to play two roles for me, a task that she performed with great pride and efficiency. Looking back now, I can only imagine the pain from her perspective. Being the mirror image of both her and my dad, and a loving symbol of their union, one cannot fathom the heartache that she must have felt having to look at one face, and constantly see two people that she loved tremendously.

My mother was everything that a child could ask for. We did everything together, from just goofing around, to her giving me simple lessons that would be essential to my development as a young man, the young man that she fully expected me to be.

Unbeknownst to us both, our time together would be short lived. Only a few years after my birth, my mother discovered that she had cancer, and that things did not look good in terms of beating it. This was a death blow to my family. My mother, the only girl out of four children, the glue for her siblings, had met an obstacle that she couldn't hurdle. Everyone poured all of their resources into finding a way to cure her, only to have everything come full circle to the original conclusion.

Our days together were numbered.

Now this is nothing short of a testament to my mother's strength and love. Even after being told that her time was short on this earth, she refused to just lie around sick. She took her money, and mustered up the strength for one last trip, telling my grandmother that this was the way she wanted me to remember her. She took me to Disney World. Can you imagine that, you have just been told that you are going to die, and you up and take your child to Disney World in an effort to provide a loving memory?

Unfortunately, that is not the last memory that I have of my mother. I remember the time that we spent together afterwards vividly. You see, her condition had gotten so bad that we had to move in with my grandmother in Maryland so that she could be taken care of. I remember her fights to maintain her lively spirit in my presence; her rapid weight loss, rendering her body to an almost skeleton-like frame; our rough-housing time slowly being cut short until it was non-existent because she couldn't be touched without causing her pain. Those are my most vivid memories.

Then it was all over. She died on July 28, 1986, leaving me alone at four years old. This would be the start of a downward spiral for me.

One of the first things that I can remember coming out of that situation was my disdain for God. I had people constantly telling me that my parents were in a "better place", but that was not how my young mind had perceived it. In my mind I was thinking, what better place could there be for parents than with their son? I knew that neither had made the choice to leave me alone, so I soon started to believe that they had been taken from me by God, since he was the one who knew it all. Though I had a pair of amazing grandparents who stepped in from day one and assumed the roles as parents, he had made me inferior to all those who had their birth parents in their lives.

The foundation for my thinking, contrary to what everyone around me was telling me, would be the gateway through which a lot of low self-esteem and bad behavior would travel through as a kid.

During my early school years, I allowed myself to be bullied due to my lack of self-love, and I harbored an inner-hatred for those around me who were truly happy. I acted out in class, receiving bad grades and all of the punishments that came along with them, only to return to school with the same attitude.

By the time I had reached middle school, things were getting worse. I had begun to experience things at home such as drugs and women from being around my uncles, and various people in my neighborhood outside. I would say that though I hadn't actually done any drugs at that point, that was my first real introduction to the street lifestyle. It was cool to me, guys outside had the ability to stay out later than me, they didn't have to go to school, they had a little bit of money, etc. I began to idolize them and certain members of my family who were also living that way as well.

This is the point where I started to make my mind up, though my actions would take a little more time.

I had successfully managed to float my way through middle school with less than impressive grades and behavior that was the direct opposite of what was expected of me. By the time I made it to high school, things were starting to change. I had begun my voyage in the streets by way of my cousin and a few friends, and began to learn how to do and sell drugs. I was an avid weed smoker, and a fan of the crack-dealing business. Like so many of you, I thought that I could maintain a balance to keep my grandmother off of my back, but I was wrong. My interest in anything other than hanging out was virtually non-existent, all I wanted to do was get away from home so that I could be who I wanted to be in the streets.

Recently during a phone conversation, my grandmother recalled the exact moment when she knew that she had "lost" me. She had told me not to leave the house one day, and when she went downstairs to do her cleaning, I had left anyway. She recalled jumping in her car with one of my uncles and a baseball bat. When she caught up with me, on my way to an area that was no good, she cut me off and tried to get me to return home with threats.

"I'm not gettin' in the car!" I told her. "I'm not a kid, you just think I am. You don't know what I do when I'm not at home!" I added, full of myself as most youngsters are.

My uncle, a believer in learning things the hard way, encouraged her to let me be, and she jumped back in her car and returned home.

"I should have hit you over the head with that bat and dragged you home! You wouldn't be who you are today." She told me recently, causing us both to laugh.

From that moment forth, my life sped up to a point where everything was almost a blur. I eventually got kicked out of high school after repeating the tenth grade, and tried two additional schools to no avail. This freed me from the last restraints that I thought I had at the time. Now I was able to be an "adult", I could hang out late nights, and move about during the day performing several nefarious deeds.

I started selling drugs such as weed and crack cocaine, as well as smoking weed and PCP, running with individuals older than me who thought that I was cool. This introduced me to several girls, giving me lessons in sex that I probably shouldn't have been learning at the time in the name of "love".

I had slowly transformed myself into some of the very people that I had wanted to be like growing up.

I had even begun to contribute to the drug problem within my own household by selling crack and weed to my uncles. There we were, under my loving grandmother's roof, them sneaking past her bedroom late nights to get to mine to buy drugs, and me waking up eager to sell them to them. I had totally lost my morals because hurting my grandmother was the last thing that I wanted to do. She was my savior, always there when I needed her, no matter what I'd done.

The lifestyle that I had chosen had fully consumed me. I was virtually without a conscience. I sold drugs to the mothers of friend's too, there were no exceptions when it came to making money, even though I was a small timer. One incident even encouraged me to try to take the life of one of my uncles over a car radio that he had stolen from me while craving for drugs. Thankfully my grandmother was able to make it home after he called from inside the bathroom, where he had locked himself in a desperate attempt to escape me.

I had allowed myself to turn into a total disappointment to not only my grandmother, but my mother as well, all because I believed that I wasn't worthy of a happy life. I put myself in countless dangerous situations in the name of "fun", and experienced many heartaches as well. I have friends that are dead. I have apathetically stood by while dudes have been beaten to within an inch of their lives, some even killed, robbed, stabbed, etc. I have even participated in many gross acts of violence for reasons that are still unclear to this day, just as many of you are currently doing.

My juvenile arrest record is about a mile long because of cocky drug arrests, and me knowing that my grandmother would always come and get me out. My brushes with the law as an adult are small in number, but that is mainly because I have been incarcerated for virtually my entire adult life. I turned eighteen in a juvenile facility, and at age twenty I was arrested and convicted of robbery and assault. I received eighteen months for the offense and after doing my time and being released, I was re-arrested after three weeks and charged with a murder in state court. While awaiting trial for this offense, I was indicted by the F.B.I. for an additional murder that would take immediate precedent over the one in state court. I haven't been home since.

Now I admit, all of this might sound pretty good on a rap song, or make a good movie, but when it is your life it's another story. If this is the way that you want to live, then the streets will get you here. I put this book together so that you could hear it straight from dudes behind the wall that this is no joke. I have more to say about my life, but I will do so later in this book. I want you to read this with your parents, classmates, teachers, friends, siblings, everyone that you can get together that may be headed the wrong way. There is nothing but truth in here, no hype, no bragging. Just men who want better for you, and are trying to do their part in showing you a better way. Read on!

Peace

Part One

For those who may be contemplating whether or not they should step into the street lifestyle, for whatever reason, this section is especially for you. It is comprised of five chapters, giving you five essential steps to take in your life early so that you can get your self on the right path, a path that is full of positive opportunities.

Chapter One

Perception, Desire, Thought.

The foundations for every action.

From: Anonymous

Decisions and Consequences

The greatest lessons are often taught by the simplest of means. We can hinder the growth process and development of the person in need of help by complicating the lessons we're trying to teach. Life itself is full of lessons. There are many consequences tied to the decisions that we make. For instance, if we drive a car through a red light, we will more than likely crash. The consequences of making the decision to drive through the red light not only caused us to crash, but could cost us our life.

There are many consequences tied to the decisions that we make.

But what if we're driving the car of life without a driver's license? What if you don't know what a red light or a yield sign means? What if you're traveling on a highway, trying to reach a particular destination, but you can't read the signs that will take you to where you're trying to go? What if the road you're traveling on is full of potholes that you keep running over because you don't know what potholes look like? What if it's very dark on the road you're traveling down and your headlights are not working?

There are many consequences tied to the decisions that we make.

When we're in a swimming pool, we usually don't consider the lifeguard until we're the ones drowning. We often ignore the flight attendant until (we are about to crash) the plane is about to crash. Life always takes on new meaning when death is knocking at our door, or when times are hard. But when things seem to be going well, we often neglect the people or things that are truly important. We can listen to a friend who we may have known for thirty days, but we totally ignore people or family members who have known us all our lives. We usually ignore the people that care most about us because of our ignorance or the contempt and disrespect that familiarity sometimes breeds. And we pay for it in the long run. And the pay value of ignorance usually ain't good. Then when reality sets in, we start kicking ourselves in the rear end, or we start drowning in self misery which usually leads to a state of depression. Untreated depression can lead to all sorts of abnormal or even insane behavior, because a depressed mind is a mind that's become diseased (dis-eased). A diseased mind can produce dangerous results.

Can we listen? Some of us never pay attention to what's being said, and sometimes we honestly don't hear it if a person is talking to us. We use all sorts of psychological blockout techniques. We look like we are interested in what's being said, but in reality we're just waiting to talk. Maybe it's because we feel that we are the only ones who have something important to say. When we speak we want everybody to listen, and when they don't we become frustrated, sometimes to the point where a simple conversation (that's if we're conversing) turns into an outright argument, or a fist fight, or worse. Many of us result to foolishness because we haven't learned or haven't been taught how to listen. Listening is an art form that is easy for some, but very hard for most of us. Do you ever say to yourself, after something bad happens to someone else, "If they would have listened, things would not have turned out that way"? Do you recall asking yourself that same question after something not so good happens to you? Sometimes we ignore ourselves. I ignore myself quite often. I also listen to myself. But I listen with reason, I ignore with reason to try to make the decisions that are good for my social development. And I often make bad decisions, but less than before because I have reason. And what is reason? 1) The cause or motive for an action, decision, or conviction; 2) The capacity for rational thinking; 3) To think or argue logically; 4) To reach a conclusion by logical thinking. And what is logic? The study of reasoning, valid reasoning. Good old fashioned common sense.

There are many consequences tied to the decisions that we make.

The knots we tie can become other people's problems. It's kind of like unconsciously setting a trap that others will fall victim to in the future. You know, like planting landmines, and not knowing it. But some people purposely plant landmines, knowing what the future effects of those landmines will be. Some form of death or destruction. When someone, or something tells you a lie that you believe to be the truth, it could be a timebomb waiting to explode. You live five days, or in some cases twenty-five to fifty years believing the lie to be truth. Then all of a sudden something happens and the truth is revealed to you. When this happens, we usually react in one of three ways, or in some instances all three: 1) We experience an emotional/psychological death and feel mentally destroyed, causing us to act out; 2) We ignore it, in which case our reason is not working and the mind is in a state of ignorance and denial, and as a result we live in misery, and/or; 3) We embrace the truth however hard it may be and grow from it, in which case we're able to move on with our lives. The knot we tie that can become other people's problems can be either telling a lie, or refusing to acknowledge the truth. Either way, it's a landmine. Some of us are walking landmines, and walking landmines are deadlier than the ones that don't move.

The decisions that we make have a thousand consequences tied to them.

1) Listening is an art, 2) Comprehension is a skill, and 3) Self-discipline is a blessing. Depending on how you use the three, they can be just the opposite. Listening without reason can alter your perception and change reality. Comprehension without logic can corrupt the decision-making process. And self-discipline without direction can have you trapped in a state of repetitive behavior that is not conducive to your mental and physical growth and development. Arrested development and retardation are similar. To arrest something means to stop, seize or hold it. When something is retarded, that means that it's progress has been impeded or slowed. Not listening, or listening without reason, can stop, seize, hold, or slow down your progress. It can also slow down the progress of others who have to give extra attention to you because you refuse to listen. Sort of like when parents have to keep taking off from work to come to your school because you're constantly getting in trouble as a result of your not listening; or when your friend tries to explain to you what you're doing that causes them and your family pain, but you don't listen. As a result, your friend leaves you, your family falls apart after you end up dead or in prison. Of course that's an extreme example, but it's reality for some people. There are a thousand consequences tied to your decisions. Everything you do will affect others, whether you want your actions to or not. Listening is an art, comprehension is a skill, and self-discipline is a blessing.

The decisions that we make have a thousand consequences connected to them.

The freedom to choose is not the same as free will. That sounds like an oxymoron, but it's not. Choice and will are two different things. Choose means to select or desire. Will, here, means the mental faculty of deciding upon a course of action. What's the difference? Choice is the act, will is the thought driving behind the act. Whoever or whatever controls the thought, dictates the act. If a person tells you something, and you believe what you've been told, then you will act on that belief. What we are told creates a desire, and desire drives the will. Words, concepts, looks, sounds, and all sorts of things, whether true or false, are seeds that are planted within our minds. Those seeds become thought, which tells us what to do or how to respond when a situation or circumstance arises. The thought will then determine the decision we make. The choice. Choice is the act, will is the thought. In the hood, if someone is acting out of character based on what someone else said to them, we'll say that the person that's acting out of character has been "siced up". Kind of like convincing a person to do something that they wouldn't do under normal circumstances, i.e. gasing a person up. The decisions that we make have a thousand consequences connected to them. Freedom to choose is not the same as free will.

There are a thousand consequences tied to the decisions that we make.

Desire feeds the will. If the transcendence of desire is the end to all suffering, as long as we desire we will suffer. Everybody suffers, it's normal. It's how we handle what we see as suffering that makes a difference in our lives. Some of us have a total breakdown, mentally and physically. And some of us find a way to use suffering as energy that fuels the building of character and go on to do great things. I don't know any sound minded person that likes to go through pain and suffering. But there is no experience that others before us have not experienced. We can learn from the experiences of others if we listen, but do we know how to listen? If we don't, we must learn how to listen. Don't wait to talk when the voice of experience is speaking to you. Can you hear me?

Decisions and Consequences.
The Struggle Continues . . . .
April, 13, 2010

From: Anonymous

To the youth,

In this life mistakes can be fatal or destructive to the one who makes them or to others. It is imperative that you not make them.

All actions in human life begin first with a decision to make them come into being. The decisions that you make in life to act or not to act govern, for the most part, how your life will go. It is paramount that these decisions which give birth to actions that will, without doubt, engender a result, whether it be a favorable or unfavorable one, be prudent and rational. Never, if possible, make a rash, imprudent decision to act. It could be the decision if you do that may result in your untimely demise, or your freedom being perpetually taken away from you.

Life is very, very fragile and temporary. Before you know it your youth will be gone and your life closer to death. You cannot afford to waste time on foolishness, unnecessary bullshit, or worthless things. Time is precious, so utilize it wisely and usefully.

The lifestyle of the "gangster" or the "thug" is useless and almost always destructive to those who indulge in it. You may think that you are slick enough, smart enough, or wise enough to avoid the almost inevitable catastrophic and woeful consequences of the lifestyle of the "thug" or "gangster", but you're not. And if you think you're strong enough to handle the consequences, or if you think you don't give a damn about them, I'm here to tell you that this is bullshit. Most of you all are not strong enough and when you're faced with tremendous adversity such as having the possibility of the rest of your life being spent behind bars, being on death row, or having a gun being thrust in your face, or a knife in your chest, you cry and ask God for help, and you regret ever having made the decisions that led to being in these predicaments. So you all need to stop faking and putting on these tough, "I don't give a fuck" facades and stay in school, graduate, and pursue careers or jobs which will bring you good income and keep you out of the bullshit that will end your lives early or take your freedom from you.

Use your minds and think prudently. Do not waste your lives. Do what you know in your heart will give you a productive life for you and your present and future family. Don't be foolish trying to be what you're not, and what is foolish to be.

Rappers who rap about living "thug" lifestyles and being "gangsters" are only trying to sell records and make money. It's all for entertainment, so don't take what they say literally and don't try to emulate what they say in reality. This is foolish, as well as perilous. I'm not telling you don't listen to rap music; there's nothing wrong with listening to it, or any other genre. But I strongly emphasize not to try to actually live what you're listening to. It's safe when art imitates life, but dangerous when life imitates art, sometimes anyway.

In Japan, the art of the culture is often violent and even depraved in Manga and Hentai, the two most lucrative and popular forms of art in Japanese society. But Japanese people rarely try to act out the art that they love and support almost fanatically. They're prudent enough and smart enough to know that if they wish to live safely, freely, and productively, they cannot act out their beloved art in real life. And this is why in Japan crime is so low, and why their society is so peaceful.

You should be smart enough to listen to whatever you want musically, watch whatever you want theatrically, etc., and not try to manifest these things in your own lives. This also goes for books. You may read something that arouses your interest or desire, but you must resist the urge to act out things that can possibly be harmful to yourselves or others. Stop being imbeciles and acting like you cannot think for yourselves, don't mess up your lives being fools! Leave "gangsterism" and "thugism" in art, i.e music, books, and movies. Do not give real life to destructive lifestyles and inclinations. Show that you are smart and not a generation of fools like a lot of the preceding generations of youths and "adults" have been, and like you as a whole are continuing to be.

It's time for you all to use your creative energy positively, even if you have to write, or rap, or make movies about negative things sometimes. Stop taking your money and spending it all on material bullshit like chains, pendants, and cars that have no value. Think real estate property, valuable artwork, stocks and bonds, jewelry that holds value and is an investment. Stop being fools!

Stop killing each other for useless reasons. Think for yourselves and don't follow fatalistic people or doctrines. Live and let live. Stop hating just to hate. Stop wasting your precious lives on things that are completely unproductive and useless. Think how you can help others in a meaningful way.

And for all of you out there that still want to be "thugs" or "gangsters", my message is this:

You all will definitely suffer hardship, stress, and a lot of other woes, so don't think you won't. And you'll find, if you're still alive, that everything you did was a big waste of time. Please though, do not sacrifice someone else to relieve your misery when it comes. Take your consequences like a honorable person. You made your bed, so lay in it by yourselves. Don't "bitch out" and snitch on someone because you can't take it. You must live with your choices. No matter what they are, or what they may bring to you, face them with courage and honor.

March 29, 2010

From: Anonymous

Beautiful Black Children Of The World

Let me start by sharing a little about myself. I'm serving a life sentence in federal prison. I've been incarcerated for the past eight years. I have a beautiful eight year old daughter in the world. I've been in jail since she was five months old. I've lost both of my grandmothers to heart attacks since I've been in jail. I've lost numerous friends, family members, and associates to the streets. Most fell victim to gun violence, and the same thing I fell victim to, prison. I was raised by my mom, my father overdosed on drugs when I was five years old. I had a brother ten years older than me that was killed when I was nine years old. I came to jail at the age of nineteen, I will be twenty-eight this October. Before this, I did numerous juvenile bits. I have four younger sisters, two of them gave birth to sons and I now have two nephews that I know of.

I'm under lock and key. My contact with my family is limited, and I live in a room that's about the size of a closet. I have people that tell me what to do, when to do it, and what time to lock in my room, not to mention what time to eat, strip off my clothes, stick out my tongue, turn around, bend over, and spread your ass! All this while others watch on. I have no privacy. I am the personal property of the Federal Bureau of Prisons. I'm what people call a modern day slave.

A lot of the decisions that I made in life created my current circumstances. As a man thinketh, so is he. Your mind is like fertile soil. The seeds you plant, will sprout into trees, and those trees will bare fruit. Whether the fruit is good or bad, depends on the seeds that you planted.

I planted negative seeds, which sprouted the fruit that I must now live off. Though it is bitter, it is the only fruit I have to survive. We are creators of our own circumstances. I neglected my education, which was my biggest mistake. I didn't hurt myself exclusively either, I hurt all of my loved ones as well. Your decisions not only affect you, but also others.

All of this pain I caused through sincere ignorance.

At one time I was all of your ages. Older people used to warn me, but I never listened. When you're young, you think you have all the answers. Sad to say, you don't have any of them. I spoke to my grandmother on the phone two days before she passed. She expressed her love for me. I could tell that she was deeply hurt because I was calling her from prison. She asked me, "Why didn't you just listen?" I had no excuses, I simply answered, "Grandma, I made my bed and now I have to lay in it." Two days later, she died.

Everything has been taken away from me. It took my experiences for me to realize what is most important to me in life. It's not those cars, clothes, and materialistic things that I sold drugs for. It's family and love. There is nothing in this world that can amount to family and love. "Life" is based on "Love". Without love, there is no life. Children have a tendency to look for love in all the wrong places. That's why a lot of them take to the streets. The love is not there though, the streets have no love for anyone. The price that you will have to pay is not worth it. The streets will cost you your life, either by death or jail. You might hear some people glorify the street life, or doing time in jail like that's supposed to make them tough. Those rappers are out there just talking. A lot of them are just children themselves. Yet, they influence ya'll with a bunch of stuff that sounds tough. That's all they're doing is talking though. They're making too much money rapping for them to be in the streets. Don't let them trick you, as if they made it by doing things the wrong way. All they are trying to do is sell records, by any means! Even if that means telling you to sell drugs, carry guns, and kill people who look just like you. You are hearing the truth from someone who was once a dedicated street soldier. I was one of the fortunate ones who didn't end up murdered in the streets, but rather made it to prison in one piece. However, I still lost my life, I am physically dead to society. I'm not in control of my life or, the life of my child.

I can't be the father that mine wasn't to me. I can't be the big brother that mine was to me. I'm just left in this box with nothing but hope. My hope is that I can get another shot at life, because I damn sure would do a lot of things different. When I was fifteen, I was arrested by an officer we called "razorhead". This officer caught me with drugs before. He confiscated them and took me home to my mother. On this particular day, he found drugs and a gun on me. He took me to a juvenile facility known as "Boy's Village". The last thing he told me was that I wasn't going to be nothing but another statistic. I never forgot those words. In my life now, I discovered the meaning to what he was trying to tell me so many years ago. I'm just another number, you kids are not! You are the future. You have the power to break the chains and really become someone of importance. Don't make the mistakes that I've made, or even attempt to walk in my footsteps. There are no happy endings to this life, just sad, real life stories of heartache and pain. I don't wish my experiences or conditions on anyone. That's why I urge you to go the right way and do what's right by your family. The wrong way is a dark gloomy street, that's certainly filled with danger and cold, lonely nights. This road leads to your demise, if you go too far down this street, you will never find your way back.

Love your family with all your heart. When your friends abandon you, which they will, and you're lost in the jungle, your family are the only people that will search for you, and try to bring you home. Children I speak from the heart, and I beg you to take my advice in stride. I hope to at least make a difference in one of your lives.

May 23, 2010

It's All In The Mind

Many people today either don't understand, or refuse to acknowledge, the importance of maintaining positive thoughts. We often allow the inception of our journeys to be polluted and counter-productively shaped by the false notions that are currently bombarding us by way of our televisions, our so-called friends, and in most cases, our physical circumstances. It is imperative, in order for us to develop positively in every aspect, that we consciously maintain a positive outlook on the future. This simple, yet profound foundation will not only ensure that your lives will rise to their highest potential, but it will also preserve your health, and give you complete control over your happiness.

As I said in the introduction, perception influences thought, and your thoughts manifest through your actions. Your actions, in case you didn't know, are the artistic hands that draw the blueprint of how your life will look once the construction process is complete. So if you begin your journey of life with a semi-analytical glance at your surroundings (or circumstances) and determine that everything is all bad, then guess what, you have just laid the foundation that will eventually govern your behavior. Your outlook on everything from relationships, to locations, to circumstances that you can associate with that initial glance, is now distorted.

Notice that I referred to your initial viewing process as a *semi*-analytical *glance*?

I did that for a reason, follow me.

Most of us are usually in such a hurry to get somewhere that we almost always end up making two mistakes, both of which can cost you dearly. The first mistake is that we fail to really *look* at, or analyze, the topic in question. This can transcend many dilemmas such as a relationship, a situation concerning money (or lack thereof), our living conditions and all they may entail, or anything else that you may can think of. Instead we *glance*, whether it be out of fear, impatience, rage because we feel as though we are owed something, or some other fallacious belief.

How can you effectively get to the root of a dilemma, or get an accurate view of your circumstances, by simply glancing at them in a hurry? It is virtually impossible, you are bound to miss something, something that may prove to be critical somewhere down the line.

The second mistake is the trickle-down effect of the first. If you are only glancing at your dilemma (or circumstances), you are only taking in the surface of what you see, not the essence. Subsequently, when your mind starts to process what you've seen, which is the analyzation process that will shape your perception, you are really setting yourself up for trouble because you are only analyzing a *fraction* of what you have encountered.

That, is semi-analyzing: Failing to look into the heart of a matter (objectively) and 1) See it for exactly what it is; 2) Determine why it exists; and 3) Figure out what you can do to improve it, without jeopardizing your development.

The two part mistake becomes whole when the process of shaping your perception is complete, or so you think. Now your thoughts will start to manufacture and nurture your intent, based on a dilemma that you allowed to mold your perception that you never took the time to understand in the first place. The crazy part is that this is just the tip of the iceberg. You see, all of this is internal, meaning it is going on inside of you, which can be dangerous in and of itself because you haven't actually *done* anything yet. You are merely choosing a path on which to travel, or drawing a blueprint on which to build on, based solely on early experiences, and what you have come to believe as a result of those experiences.

When you take the time to analyze what you have just read, it can be a bit scary I guess. At the same time, these very words should spark some excitement somewhere inside of you because they prove that *you*, not a situation or another person, have all of the power. It is all in how you see things, and how you see yourself, that will enable you to draw an effective blueprint for your life.

Some people are unfortunate enough to have tragic experiences bestowed upon them, others go through things that some would consider mild bumps and bruises, but neither should allow these things to spawn irrational behavior. Life is no bed of roses, as the great Nelson Mandela once said, so you need not expect every day to be warm and sunny; and every road to be smooth and light-free. The quicker you realize this, the easier it will be for you to do away with the excuses that we tend to use in an attempt to justify foolish decisions. Don't hold on to disappointments over failures that do not belong to you, this only causes you to get in your own way, otherwise known as an excuse. "I'm a product of my environment, this is all I know!" These types of things. We have all heard them, and most of us have used them quite often.

The truth of the matter is that if your thoughts aren't right, chances are that your life won't be right either. Everyone has an energy, or a vibe, that they put out into the universe unconsciously. This energy can only be one of two things, positive or negative. The basic law of attraction ensures that you will be surrounded, in every aspect, by the very energy in which you put out. If you are a negative person, you will emit negative energy, and therefore find yourself surrounded by negative people. They may not necessarily be negative toward you directly, but the actions from their own lives will surely bring residual negativity to yours. If you keep a positive attitude, even in the face of adversity, then you will emit an energy that will surely allow you to reap the benefits that you deserve.

The key is patience, coupled with good old fashioned hard work.

We often want things to happen at that very moment when we submit our request, failing to grasp the idea that everything happens in due time. An older individual once told me that the immediate is often the enemy of the ultimate. Think about that for a moment. When you juxtapose whatever you may be going through at the moment, with where you will end up down the line if you think positive, that statement should be just as profound to you as it is to me to this day.

No matter where you may have to start from, or who tells you that you can only do this, or you can't do that, always keep a positive outlook on your present situation. Those things that are meant to tear you down should only add steam to the engine that powers your dreams. With maximum effort and a steadfast commitment, things will get better. You will experience heartaches and setbacks, and they will tempt you to entertain thoughts of stepping outside of the law, but it is on you to *fully* analyze the decision that you may find yourself contemplating.

Is it worth it? Can you take a few bullets, or a life sentence, or both, and honestly be able to say that you had no other way?

You will be older far longer than you will be younger, so why not work hard in the beginning so that you and those that you love will be able to play harder in the end? It would be foolish to have to spend the majority of your life paying dire consequences for a decision that you made on impulse instead of thinking it through, only to look back in hindsight and discover that you made it out to be more than it really was.

It doesn't matter that I am the author of this book, or that I know the people in it who chose to share their wisdom with you, we are all students in life. I learned something from, and saw the correlation in each letter comprised in every chapter. The brothers in this one are all trying to show you that thought is key to both failure and success, and that you must take the time to weigh your options. Are your thoughts laying the blueprint that will build you a platform that will afford you the opportunity to present a solution to the problems that you wish to escape from? Or are you simply on the verge of multiplying them? Every decision has a consequence, no matter how small you may think it is.

In his letter, the first brother offered a plethora of things to think about. Here are a few that I took from it: 1) There are many consequences tied to the decisions that we make; 2)

Untreated depression can lead to all sorts of abnormal behavior because a depressed mind is a mind that has become dis-eased; 3) Many of us result to foolishness because we haven't been taught how to listen.

The second brother taught the following: 1) All actions in human life begin first with a decision to make them come into being; 2) The decisions that you make in life to act or not to act, govern how your life will go; 3) You must think for yourself, rather than follow fatalistic people or doctrines.

The third brother tied it all together to form a collective message from three separate perspectives. He stated: 1) The decisions that he made created his current circumstances; 2) As a man thinketh, so is he; 3) Your mind is like fertile soil, the seeds that you plant will sprout into trees and those trees will bear fruit, whether bitter or sweet is up to you.

The underlying point, as you can see from those examples, is the importance of rational thinking. Things are rarely as bad as they look. In fact, how you see things might be part of the problem!

Do not hurl yourself into the point-of-no-return-zone by doing something stupid like selling drugs. Putting yourself in a position to be shot, robbed, killed, or locked up, just so you can afford to buy the clothes that you see some of your favorite stars wear on television is a grave mistake. You will feel way beyond stupid later down the line, if you make it that far, when you find out that many of them had jobs when they were your age. Realistically, they are working at that very moment where they are projecting the false images that heavily influence you to try to follow in what you believe to be their footsteps.

Stop and think before you make a huge scene over a minor issue for the sake of gaining a reputation. If you haul off and punch this guy in the face for cool points, and he falls and hits his head in a manner that causes death, can you sit back in a cell with a sentence that will propel you well into your adult years and say that it was really that serious?

Don't put yourself in a sticky situation that will follow you forever. Keep your thoughts positive so that positive things will come your way, that way you will be less likely to be tempted to do something crazy in the form of a short cut. Let everyone that tries to encourage you to do wrong have the moment, you analyze and prepare for the future. You know what is right and what is wrong, but if you refuse to listen to yourself, you have no chance of hearing anyone else.

Chapter Two

Strive to be the reason,

not the result.

From: Anonymous

Brothers and Sisters,

I am twenty-six years of age and I'm currently serving a life plus 135 years sentence. I chose to take this opportunity and time to help you see and understand the importance and value of your life here on earth, and the easiest ways to destruction if you don't not only love and respect yourself, but life and the laws of it. Let me begin with assuring you that no matter how and what you think, you are definitely here for a purpose. When I was growing up, there was no way that I could believe that it was a purpose for me being here. In my earliest years, I didn't have it too easy. I didn't come up in a stable home that consisted of a mom, dad, etc. I lived with pretty much everybody, family wise. Despite the fact that I desired to live with both mom and dad, it just didn't happen that way. My mother was addicted to drugs for a large portion of my younger years. Not understanding this as a child, being lied to, and wondering why I couldn't really see my mother, took me through some really hard times. It is not until now, that I really understand how damaged mentally and emotionally I became by having to go through that. I began running away from home when I was eleven years old. The only way to describe my feelings at the time is simply, nothing. I guess that I had cried and became so upset until I became numb. Of course I got caught and brought home, but I kept leaving everytime I got the chance. So you can say that I pretty much lived in the streets from age twelve to eighteen. During my time living in the streets, I experienced things that a child my age had no business experiencing, ranging from assaults to murder. The streets are for no one. In a young and immature state of mind, the streets are everything that you've ever dreamed of. But let me tell you this, they are nothing of the sort unless you enjoy nightmares. The streets are heartless, soulless, lifetaking, and the equivalent to hell. It is all an illusion.

Now if you look at the things that I've been through, and the age that I went through them, you may say to yourself that it was justifiable. I too thought this way for a long time, but sisters and brothers, there is no way to justify you contributing to your own mental and physical death. So you might ask, what were you supposed to do? Everybody has a purpose in life. At this point, I don't know exactly what I was to do, but I went through it and now I'm here to inform you that you don't have to do the same. Let me be the example that turns you in a better direction. I may have done exactly what I was intended to do, only God knows.

So to all of my young brothers, let me be the example for you. Stay focused, never let your emotions overpower your intelligence. I understand that some of us aren't fortunate enough to have a perfect family like we desire, but be strong. God is with you. He said that there will be struggle, but ease shall follow. I don't know all of your options, but I chose the streets and now I'm in prison serving a life sentence. So there is definitely a better way.

And to all of my sisters, I know it's rough out there, but a lot of you have it all wrong. You are all priceless. I sit and observe, and a lot of you sisters have reduced yourselves to material beings. You will never be satisfied this way. You are not "things", so things will never be able to satisfy you alone. I value my sisters. You are the mother of creation. You have to be more respectful of yourselves, and more respect shall follow. I see my sisters all over the world in all kind of unnecessary situations stemming from relationships. Get your priorities in order. I'm definitely not speaking against you having a relationship, but establish yourselves mentally and emotionally.

In conclusion, I just want to stress that I honestly love all of my brothers and sisters. I've been given the opportunity to view life and everything in it for what it really is. It is most important that you respect and honor your elders. Education is just as important also. Knowledge and understanding are both vital tools for your own salvation. Love yourself, and never sell yourself short. Life is most definitely what you make it.

And for all of those who feel that the streets are the route to take, then just understand what you are selling yourself to. What might seem like fun for the time being, will quickly change in your face for the worst. The streets are no doubt the road to destruction, no way around it. I've already witnessed it for you. I had to learn the hard way because I didn't believe it could happen to me, but as I mentioned many times before, there is purpose to your life and if you are acting against that purpose, God will bring you to an end one way or another. I can go on forever, but you should have gotten the point by now. It's very simple, the so called "street life" is no life at all. As quickly as it starts, it will surely end. You are here to fulfill one purpose only, and that is to serve your humble and heavenly nature in which we all were created. Anything contrary to that, it's all bad. I'm going to leave you with that. I love you sisters and brothers just as much as I've had the opportunity in coming to love myself. God willing, we'll have the chance to talk more. Take care. Love, patience, and time.

May 16, 2010

From: Anonymous

Reflecting upon my past usually rehashes the familiar memory of a disillusioned reprobate. As a youth, I exemplified the characteristic traits of a socially engineered product of my environment. Like most of my peers, I was ignorant of my purpose and held an obscure understanding of self. This vague perception inevitably lead me to emulate my neighborhood mentors who were themselves in an execrably deteriorated state of mind. Beyond a shadow of a doubt, I indubitably thought that this savage way of life was the right way to live until I found myself surrounded by concrete and steel within the abode of Terre Haute Federal Penitentiary.

Upon observing my deplorable surroundings in prison, I realized that an overwhelming ninety-percent of us were brainwashed buffoons. We were hopelessly consumed by sports and entertainment, while erroneously professing ourselves to be pimps and gangsters.

This particular mental state blinded us all, and now we are getting pimped by a corporate gangster who capitalized off of our ignorance in a legal capacity.

From that point on, I developed an insatiable lust for knowledge, and an overwhelming desire to resurrect myself from the deadly grave of the mentally dumb, deaf, and blind. What are you going to do with your life while you still have a chance?

May 15, 2010

From: Anonymous

It's Not A Game!

To our future who thinks being tough is cool, let me tell you a little about where I come from and how I lived. Coming up I had nothing, but wanted everything living in a three bedroom apartment with thirteen people living there in S.I, New York.

But anyway, that's just to give you a little about how I started out.

More or less, the reason I'm writing this kite (letter) is to get you to understand that just because you don't have nothing does not mean that you have nothing to care about or live for in this world. You are only what you make yourself out to be. So, if you ain't shit, when you look in the mirror, you won't see shit. To be honest, we are all more than what we think. Sometimes we just need to take the time to sit back and evaluate ourselves, and then take the necessary steps to change our life for the good we all have in us.

Education is the most powerful weapon any person can have, along with self respect, love, discipline, integrity, and ambition. The order goes to each is own.

As far as friends, some have ulterior motives for you. They say that they have love for you but watch and encourage you to stray the wrong way. A real friend will only want to see you do right, trust that because being far away from home and loved ones hurts, and it often hurts your loved ones more than it hurts you.

So always remember that life is not a game when you're the one sitting in a cell on Death Row in Terre Haute, Indiana. I hope you take heed, so you won't have to get turned upside down in order to learn how to live right side up.

June 12, 2010

You Have A Purpose

Everyone, no matter what your race, fiscal situation, genetical make-up, or geographic location is, has a purpose for their life. Let's just get that out into the open right now for those who may feel otherwise.

As you have just read from each of the three brothers in this chapter, belief in the opposite is one of the biggest misconceptions that can easily drive a young person into the waiting, open arms of the criminal lifestyle. You see, contrary to what some may believe, turning to crime isn't always about needing materials. In fact, many young people surround themselves with the criminal element with absolutely no intentions of actually committing a crime. Most of the time it is simple recognition that they desire, the need to feel that heavy cloak of invisibility lifted from their existence.

Nobody, no matter who you are, likes to be ignored.

Coming up in some of these low-income, and now even middle class neighborhoods, young people are constantly seeing images of what they have come to believe that life is about in the streets, regardless of what they are being taught at home. Sure, they see the people that are labeled criminals wearing clothes that most parents can't even pronounce, and some even witness the extremes to which they are willing to go in order to not only acquire said materials, but also maintain the overall lifestyle, but unfortunately that is not what initially resonates.

What shines the most in their eyes is the attention that they see guys receive from their peers, the spotlight, what is often mistook for love.

This, in their minds, makes everything else worthwhile.

To offer a different perspective, it's sort of like when a mother forces herself not to curse out her boss, even though she feels that a line has been crossed. Instead she takes it on the chin because she enjoys seeing the smile on her child's face at the end of the week when she is able to buy him/her something that he/she has been asking about. That simple smile gives the mother a purpose, it serves as the motivation that drives her to get up every morning and bite her tongue, and to even deny herself something that she may want or need on payday. It all comes full circle when she sees her child happy, producing the smile that always shines light at the end of the tunnel that is the previous week.

For a kid however, things are not that simple. Doing the right thing doesn't bring the kind of recognition that guys in the streets get applauded for. To garner that kind of "love", you have to get out there and put in the work, which is counterproductive to your purpose.

The first brother offered his past as a fine example of this very point. For him, the streets satisfied his craving for family stability. Being shuffled around as a youth, it almost seemed as though nobody cared if he came or went until he found the streets, or rather they found him. From that initial point of recognition, it became about doing what was necessary in order to maintain his importance, something that I can personally relate to. All of the things that we experienced as young people, like many of you will surely face if you choose our path, paled in comparison to the joy that most of us felt when we discovered that whenever we left for the day, people wanted to know when we were coming back. The binding factor was that these people, some who appeared to be more "together" than us, shared our same feelings of hopelessness and unimportance.

That was the spark that was needed, the feeling of purpose that would later be the excuse that we would use in an attempt to justify all that we would do as the years went by. However, at the opposite end of the spectrum, we were totally oblivious to the fact that, like that officer told Brother Jay in chapter one, we were also on the path to becoming statistics.

I believe that the second brother said something that was both raw, and profound at the same time. In his letter he said: "If you look in the mirror and you don't see shit, you won't be shit!", or something to that effect. If I could put things into perspective in one sentence, that is exactly what I would say. It doesn't take anyone else to validate your existence or carve your path in this life, it all starts with *you* and what *you* want to do.

Your self-esteem level can greatly affect your overall outlook on what your purpose is. It is essential that you put yourself first. Firm belief in whatever it is that you believe is your purpose is what will give you the strength to weather the storm that is other people's opinions. If you have a dream, no matter what it is, and you have people constantly taking shots at it directly or subliminally, the logical thing for a young mind to do would be to defer the dream because it will never happen, or so we're told. This is something that our young people face from all sides. Whenever it is time to choose what they feel is their calling in life, and they choose sports, or God-forbid, rap, people immediately start to hammer their dreams with stereotypes and dogmatic opinions. It is important that you stay committed because people are always going to say something, especially when they encounter something in it's infant stages.

The criticism, and sometimes ostensible hatred that you will receive should serve as motivation, fueling you to make them all believers of your purpose whether you want to be a teacher, a basketball player, a rapper, or a construction worker. You keep it planted firmly in your mind that none of these titles define you. Just as the first brother realized about some of his early experiences, as well as his current plight, they are just a means for you to be able to serve your true purpose.

With that said, you must be willing to work hard and let your labor defend your chosen profession, not your mouth. It's all about action. You lend credibility to people's opinions when you misuse your platform, or mis-represent yourself in front of others by doing foolish things that garner negative attention. This is simply you assisting in tearing down your own platform that enables you to perform your service.

Is everyone's purpose related? This is a question that was posed to me recently.

I believe so.

Though the means by which you serve your purpose may vary, the fundamental purpose of all of us is to inspire each other, to help the next person in need somehow. Famous poet, and phenomenal woman, Maya Angelou once said: "You cannot go through life with a catcher's mitt on both hands, you must give back." What an extraordinary statement. No matter who or where you are, we all possess the innate ability to turn on a small light in a dark room. This can be done through any profession or circumstance, you don't have to be on television to do it, it doesn't matter what you're wearing, or how you look, nor does money govern it.

If you stopped to give a homeless man the jacket off of your back, he's not going to say: "Oh no, I can't accept this because you don't have on the latest Air Jordan sneakers, or you have dreadlocks, or you're not my color!"

No.

He's going to be thankful that you cared enough to sacrifice something that was your's, whether you paid for it or not, so that he could be warm.

If you felt that your purpose in life was to help families in danger of foreclosure, and you went to a woman who was about to be kicked out of her home, she wouldn't say: "Why doesn't your purse match your heels?", or "I haven't seen you around here before.", or "No thanks, you had a baby out of wedlock."

Of course not.

In fact, those very things, should they be true, may be something that the two of you have in common, allowing you to forge an immediate bond that takes the edge of embarrassment off.

Those are just two examples, but the moral of this chapter is this:

All that you may have endured up to this point, was tailored just for you. If it already hasn't, it will someday lend the needed credibility to who you will become when it is time for you to service the world, one person at a time. No matter how you may have started, you are not the victim. You were blessed with early experience, as well as proof that the world is no bed of roses.

Your purpose will be served, whether you want it to or not, so you might as well follow your dreams and do it on your own terms. The only person that can shut down your plan is you.

All three of the brothers in this chapter, as well as myself, would love to be having this conversation with you as free men, but unfortunately we chose to do things our way, or so we thought. Now we have to suffer all of the woes that come with the plight of incarceration, only to have everything come full circle and be here sharing what we have been through with you in an effort to inspire you to push through that maze that you might be in right now, so that you can come out on the right side.

Maybe this was our purpose all along, you never know.

Chapter Three

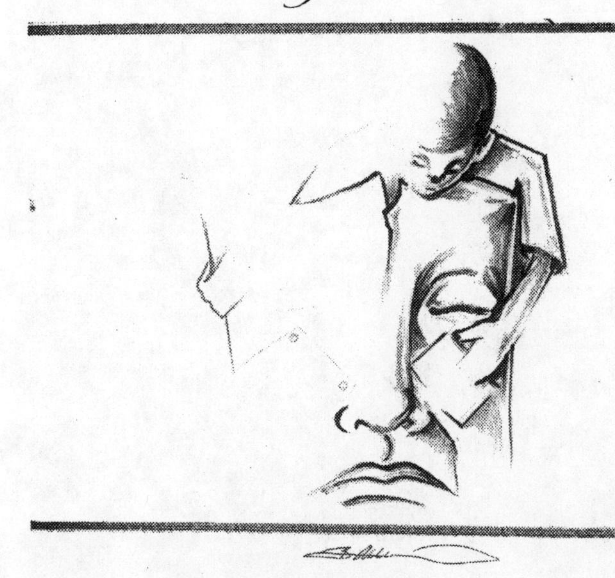

Understand that you are unique,
then take the necessary steps to prepare for your future.

From: Anonymous

If I had to use one word to describe my mentality, when I was living a troubled life, it would have to be lost. I couldn't make heads or tails of anything. At the root of my problem was my lack of self-love, discipline, direction, accountability, ambition, and basic life skills. I know now that those are essential to being a responsible adult. That is why I am taking this opportunity to explain how these deficiencies translate into a life of crime and deviant behavior.

Direction

There is an old African proverb that goes: "If you don't know where you are going, any road will get you there." I had no direction in my life. I had no five or ten year plan. I didn't have a one day plan! I never awoke with a goal in mind. I chose my activities recklessly and spontaneously. That is why my activities ended up getting me in so much trouble. I didn't understand that productive and responsible people have goals and that their days are carefully planned out because they are working towards something. I preferred to waste time running the streets, doing drugs, and taking things that didn't belong to me. While others were doing homework and preparing for college, I was getting high and committing crimes. I was the grasshopper who played all summer while the hardworking ant prepared for the winter. Another side effect of not having any direction is that you end up associating with others who have no direction; and there is nothing worse than a group of people with idle hands. Those that I associated with were more than encouraging when it came to my criminal activities. However, none of them gave me any meaningful advice or encouraged me to go to college, or to get a career. It is no surprise that everyone of us ended up in the prison system.

Discipline

I had no moral integrity or ethical code. I only abided by one rule; serve thyself. I did whatever I wanted, and showed no restraint. The little bit of money I had I spent so fast that I can't even remember where it went. Without discipline, you end up drowning yourself in excess. Discipline is what keeps us from being controlled by emotions, irrational thoughts, greed, and lust.

Accountability

One of my worst problems was my failure to accept responsibility for my life. I blamed all of my problems on others, i.e. my parents, my teachers, police, the world. What I didn't realize is that when you don't hold yourself accountable, you give up control of your destiny. Not taking responsibility for your life means that you have decided to let others make your decisions. That is exactly what prison is, a place where you go to have your decisions made for you. They tell you when to eat, when to recreate, when to lock up, what you are allowed to have, who can visit you, and when you can go home, if you are lucky enough to have a release date or somewhere to call home. Autonomy is a privilege that can and will be taken away from those who abuse it.

Ambition

The successful people in this world all have ambition. They have a desire to be the best at what they do. Never settle for mediocrity. There is always room for improvement in your life.

Also know that success in your career should not be your only ambition. You should also strive to be successful in your family life, or in serving your community. All this may seem to be a lot, but that is what ambition is all about. It's about being great.

Basic Life Skills

When I was growing up, I wasn't taught any life skills. I wasn't taught how to cook for myself. I wasn't taught how to write a check or balance a budget. I wasn't taught how to conduct myself in a job interview, or how to apply for college. Life skills are very important. You need to learn them at an early age. Tell your parents to take you along with them when they pay bills. Get in the kitchen with your parents, grandparents, aunts, uncles, and help them cook. Find a practice partner for job interviews and listen to their constructive criticism. Learn how to take care of yourself.

Self-Love

This is the most important. Self-love is what keeps us wanting the best for ourselves. When you lack self-love, you accept abuse from yourself and others. The lack of self-love is what leads to drug abuse, abusive friendships, abusive relationships, unfulfilling careers, and unhealthy living. Look inside yourself, find out what you like about yourself, and hold on to that. Let that be your strength when you are feeling down or when someone else is trying to tear you down. No one else should ever be able to change how you feel about yourself. However, you must always remember that in order to love thyself, you must know thyself.

I was locked up one month after my 19th birthday. I have been incarcerated my entire adult life. Now I may never see the freeworld again. I will never experience fatherhood. I have nieces and nephews I have never met. I haven't hugged or kissed my mother in over a decade, and I haven't seen her in over five years. These are only my hardships. Think about the tears my mother cries because she will never get to hug her son again, or the tears she cries because her son will die in the penitentiary. Your consequences for your actions are only half of the equation. Most of us don't consider how our behavior affects our loved ones.

The criminal lifestyle is a selfish one, because criminals are so self-absorbed we end up in prison spending the rest of our life alone with our favorite person; the man in the mirror. That is what happens to the mentally lost in the wilderness.

June 5, 2010

From: Anonymous

If there was ever a regret that I've had about my life, it would be not taking advantage of all of the good opportunities that were before me, and not realizing my potential in life earlier.

So many times, we get caught up in what we believe is how life should be, that we never take advantage of education, good role models, and all the other things that can make life the way that we want it to be. So many people live life and never reach their full potential because they never take the time to know themselves. So with that said, if you don't know what you are capable of, how can you reach your full potential?

What I've learned is that it is never too late to take advantage of the opportunities that come your way. You just have to be open-minded enough to step out of the box, and courageous enough to go out on a limb and seize it. The longer one lives, the more experience they get that will allow them to be more creative and open to reaching their full potential.

If there was one thing that I could say to someone this way, it would be: 1) Understand that you have a choice, so choose wisely; and 2) Never limit yourself to your version of life. If you limit yourself to what you know, you will never be able to see all of the possibilities that lie before you.

From: Anonymous

Throughout my life I was always called stubborn or hard-headed. So I understand the futility of telling someone who doesn't want to change: "Don't do this and don't do that!", but the opportunity to impart some knowledge that I learned the hard way is one that I can't pass up. When you're young, you can get caught up in believing that you know everything, or that you have all the time in the world to learn it eventually. I tell you straight up, you are wrong! Putting off for tomorrow what you should do today will only leave you with regrets. Doing something with your life takes work, but truth be told, so does screwing it up. So which one would you rather make an effort at doing? You can sit around making excuses about why things are bad for you and go do something illegal because you think it's easier to make money that way, but later you will realize that if you're too lazy to be a success legally, more than likely that will still be the case when you try the alternative route.

As for the lucky few that do have some success, realize that once it ends you will see that the price was way too high, and the reward is only a bunch of memories that can't do jack to help you out of your current predicament. Now, you can continue along that path, or you can make your mom proud so that when someone asks about her child she can answer with pride, instead of embarrassment.

Of course the road is hard, but it is nowhere near impossible. You have to make sacrifices to stay home and do your homework? Big deal! I look back on my life now and wish I would have made small sacrifices when I was free so that I could go to college and make something of myself, rather than getting shot at, making a little bit of money, and going to jail in the end, only to be left with nothing.

Remember one thing though when you do decide to do the right thing. Keep in mind that just because you decide to change, that doesn't mean that the world is going to change with you. An old African proverb says: One does not cross a river without getting wet. If you were living your life as a liar and a cheat on Thursday, and you decide to change, that doesn't mean that everyone is going to trust you on Friday. It takes twice as much work to repair a relationship that's tarnished, so don't be discouraged if it's tough. Also make realistic goals for your future, ones that are honestly achievable. If you dropped out of high school, don't think that you'll be the chairman of Microsoft next summer. You don't get to the top of the mountain by starting at the top.

There is no harm in adding to your original goal, helping you witness success as your dreams grow, just stay persistent.

I hope that this will help those who want to help themselves. I wouldn't want this curse of an existence put on my worse enemy because what really hurts in the end is not that you let your family and loved ones down, or the fact that the friends that you turned your back on your true friends and family for betrayed you to save their own skin or forgot about you altogether. No. It's the realization that with a few simple changes in your life, all of this could've been avoided!

March 22, 2010

From: Anonymous

Dear Brothers and Sisters,

IN THE NAME OF ALLAH, THE BENEFICENT, THE MOST MERCIFUL. I BEAR WITNESS THAT THERE IS NO GOD BUT ALLAH, AND THAT THE PROPHET MUHAMMAD IS HIS MESSENGER. AS'SALAAMU ALAIKUM.

I currently reside on federal death row in Terre Haute, Indiana. I have had the unfortunate experience of being here for seventeen years, which is almost half of my life, and the majority of my adult life. I received my death sentence at the tender age of twenty-three, and I will turn forty in a few months, Inshallah. So, it is with a heart of humility and reflection that I come before you.

After months of making excuses for why not to share my life experiences, I realized that I was doing what I have always done. I was making up excuses to justify running from my responsibilities and living beneath my best. To be honest with you, I'm down right sick and tired of running, and living in pain. So today I have chosen to stop running and plant my feet firmly in being part of the solution, and not the further destruction of my people. Although I am no longer actively doing harm to others, I've come to realize that by not sharing what little wisdom I have learned along the way, I would be complicit nonetheless.

As I choreograph my thoughts to you, I'm cognizant of the behavioral precedent that I've set which led me to this cold death row cell. Unfortunately, this moral turpitude is the only light that most people have seen me in, and for a lot of years, the only darkness that I believed I could live in. See I had bought into the narrative of others that I couldn't be anything of value and in my belief, I set out to live a de-valued life. I lived up to every negative stereotype of the black man that I knew of. I had my first child at the young age of fourteen, and what's so crazy about this is not the mere fact that I was having sex in the first place, but rather that I had become a father after my first time. Well, in name only because I had no clue as to how to raise a baby when I was still a baby myself. My son's mother, who by the way was only thirteen, was no exception.

Thanks to God, I had responsible parents that cared for my son until I was able to do so myself. I will always be grateful to them for this, but I will forever regret what happened to the dreams of both my son's mother and my own. Before we made the irresponsible choice to lose our virginity and unbeknownst to us, our dreams as well, she was a straight A student. As to be expected, not long after our son was born, the responsibilities of being a young mother became overwhelming to say the least. Add to her burdens the fact that for the first six months I denied that the baby was mine, and you can only imagine the shame that she endured. In the end it all proved to be too much for her and she dropped out of school, spending the subsequent years having many more children and depending on the government to provide for them all.

This is one of the unfortunate consequences of young sex.

This one seemingly benign lustful act, changed the course of its two participants lives so dramatically that the repercussions are still being felt twenty-five years later.

As a child I never would have assumed that such pleasure could bring with it so much pain, but this is the paradoxical nature of sex . . .

My dear brothers and sisters, it is only out of the existential confrontation with death that I stopped making excuses and believing in the low expectations set for me, and put my life in it's proper perspective by appropriately balancing my values.

So after years of traversing the winding memories of my past experiences, and the expectations of my future ones, thoughts began germinating in me that ultimately compelled me to share my journey into real manhood with you. I'm not talking about that keep it real nonsense that has us living with bipolar tendencies, contradictions and dependencies on our superficial needs that puts us in conflict with God's word, or the coercive, univocal choices that become ethically offensive to our relationship with Allah.

Our demands to be a part of something, demands us to submit to our own desires at any cost. To have the freshest materials, we're willing to debase ourselves at any cost, be it selling drugs, murder, selling ourselves, robbing, or stealing from loved ones . . . The list goes on and on.

So in my attempt to think proleptically, conjuring up questions and solutions that will heal us as a people. I offer the following . . .

If there is to be any hope for us, we must go beyond the ideological conditions that have us unconsciously adopting self-defeating habits that are detrimental and prejudicial to our future. What do I mean by this? I mean that we have to stop selling death and low self worth to our children through our entertainment! Please know that we've been led down a painful road, a road with no real purpose or moral compass, and we are continuing to pave that very road for those after us. We've allowed our children's role models to be the very people that are doing them the most harm. In a real sense, they have been allowed to raise a whole generation on sex, drugs, and violence. How can we really be surprised at the prison incarceration rate being so high when it pertains to people of color? It's a damn shame that our people, our own people, have made drug dealing, killing, and risky sex, seem so fair-seeming. I realize that some children are not blessed to have responsible parents in the household raising them. My children are such children. However, by the good graces of Allah, thus far all of my children have grown into productive, law abiding adults. I wouldn't allow them to make excuses for why they couldn't do the right thing for themselves. I realized early on in my incarceration that the absence of a positive man in the home can often mask the ubiquitous, underlying factors of persistent poverty, and malnutrition of the spirit. So via the years, I've acquired a peculiar visceral intelligence, dedicated to the survival of my families mind, body, and spirit. I've educated myself in the arts of socio-economics, political theory, revolutionary warfare, and spiritual development in order that my children would never be able to make an excuse for why their lives didn't turn out as they wished.

My children know the power of choice. They know that at the end of the day, our lives are defined by the sum of our choices and it is up to us to make the responsible one, or the irresponsible one if you can live with it. No one is responsible for our actions but us, which is why I can't complain about the plight of my life as it currently stands. I don't have any excuses for why I chose the lifestyle that I did. I can't say that I wasn't exposed to a moral way as a kid, because I was. In fact, I was raised by two hard working, law abiding, God fearing parents, and had a host of extended family support. Although I had a family structure in place, it was dysfunctional nonetheless. I didn't have to go out and find violence in the streets, it found me at home.

So because of the influences of my early conditioning and programming that I unwittingly adopted through my formative years, I know how easy it is for those of us that come from malnourished environments of seemingly perpetual failures to see our families failures through the prism of manifested destiny, or normality. If by chance you have bought into the notion that your life has to be filled with failures because of your family's history, or the community in which you are raised in, I want to dispel that notion right here and now.

With CHOICE as my template, let me give you the meaning of the word . . .

Choice: The power or opportunity of choosing; Option; The best part . . .

It's crucial to your development that you believe in your power to be whomever you want to be, against all odds. The odds that come with not having a father in your life, or a mother for that matter; the odds that come with not attending a nourished school; the odds of making it out of a rough neighborhood without being influenced by a negative light, etc.

I want you to know that despite all that says that you shouldn't be able to make it, you can. In fact, those of us that ended up in prison, on drugs, uneducated, or dead before our time are the real exceptions to the rule. Although you're led to believe that only a few of us blacks make it out of the so-called hood, it's only a myth, the same ideological conditioning that I spoke of earlier. The vast majority of people of color are educated, family orientated, God-fearing and loving, patriotic, and capable of doing anything that any other group of people claim to be able to do.

To quote one of my favorite philosophers, James Allen: "By changing my beliefs, I change who I am . . ."

The source that governs my life, The Holy Qur'an says: "God does not change the condition of a people until they change what is in their souls." (13:11)

To quote another one of my favorite philosophers, Dr, Wayne Dyer: "Our failings, too, can mark a new beginning and become a source of inspiration for our success, provided we meet them with a proper attitude and see them with the right perspective . . ."

It is in the spirit that I've worked hard to shed my once contumacious state of mind. I had to shed my proverbial old skin of ignorance in order to have a chance at true redemption and be able to reach my full potential here on death row. Like most convicts, I'm a high school dropout and a functioning illiterate, but I'm not using that as an excuse. Instead I'm using it as my motivation. If they will not provide me with access to an education, then it is up to me to do like those in third-world countries and get mine by any means necessary! They seem to have forgotten that education means freedom.

I want to encourage you to be open-minded on your journey by changing the optics in which you have chosen to see things. I recently had the opportunity to use this wisdom in relations to the brother that asked me to be a part of his efforts to bring about solutions to the problems that our people continue to struggle with. Where I saw myself as not having anything of value to add to the solution, he saw my worth and in doing so, allowed me to have another opportunity at redemption.

I share this with you in hopes that you will realize that you're surrounded by people that are willing to invest in your future, but because of the narratives of those who wish you destruction, you've been sold out as to what success looks like. You fail to see the real role models in your everyday life such as the teachers, the fire-fighters, the coaches, ministers, honor roll students in high school and college, and the everyday people that simply get up and work hard everyday to take care of their families the best that they can. These are the true role models.

My dear friends, it's time for us to collectively take a look, soberly and deeply, upon the values and behavior that result from the perspective of power as external. I believe that true power comes from knowing that with God, all things are possible, and that is only known from within. Look within yourself and choose responsibility.

"By the time! Surely man is in loss, except those who believe and do good, and exhort one another to the truth, and exhort one another to patience." (Surah: 103)

May Allah bless you and your affairs. Life life abundantly.

February 22, 2011

Self-Love

Do you love yourself?

Although that question may come off as a rhetorical one, please do not dismiss it as so because I can assure you that it is very important. Take a few minutes to actually ponder before you respond to yourself.

If your response is yes, I want you to take an additional few moments to look back in retrospect at your life leading up to this point. Can you honestly say that your actions actually support that belief?

If your answer is no, then you deserve an applause. That honest answer, which is sometimes harder than one may think, has actually placed you on the path that will lead you toward evolution.

We as a whole often look at self-love from the wrong perspective, usually deriving from our early social programming. It isn't just about being able to look in the mirror and appreciate what you see physically. Self-love has many facets, or layers, that work to determine, and demonstrate, it's authenticity. For me in particular, there are three things that come to mind whenever I ponder on the subject of self-love. I will try my best to convey my thoughts clearly as I walk you through each one, starting with the obvious.

Self-love. Everything starts with you, period. As I expressed in every chapter preceding this one, if you don't have yourself right, everything that surrounds you will be wrong. Things are no different here. Self-love is about the overall big picture, your actions not only toward others, but toward yourself as well. After all, the two go hand in hand right? How you view and treat yourself will yield how the next person will be treated when they come in contact with you.

Too often we contradict what we say with what we do, oftentimes right after we say it. For example, we all want to demand respect, but we will often try our hand at intentionally disrespecting the next person, be it via verbal semantics in the form of sly innuendoes, or outright physical gestures. Then, once we are exposed, we usually feign surprise or outrage in an effort to manufacture an excuse for a foolish reaction that was really our intention in the first place. We have all done it for one reason or another, so the point here is not to judge anyone. The point is to determine why we do it, because examples like the one that I just gave, only show that the problem lies within us.

Hurt people—hurt people, which usually comes full circle and stops with them hurting themselves. Whatever your problem is, whether you don't like something about yourself, or something about your life, you have to be willing to go within, as deep as you need to, to discover what it is. It is then, and only then, that you will place yourself on the path to loving yourself. If you don't, then you are going to become a walking landmine as Brother Menes described in chapter one, a detriment to not only yourself, but others as well. This opens the door for you to get hurt in a number of different ways, either physically, emotionally, or if you're a little older and trying to establish yourself in the work field, career-wise.

Self-caretaking. This is perhaps the biggest contradiction for most street dudes, and those who are considering that lifestyle. One of the basic principles of life for us as human beings is self preservation, or in keeping in line with the theme of this section, self-caretaking. If you love yourself, you are going to keep yourself out of situations where you know that you will get hurt, or worse. Well, at least that is the idea.

In an effort to come up with an example of our warped perception of self-preservation, or self-caretaking, I came up with the following. I recently spent a few hours juxtaposing us as human beings, the supposed smartest species on the planet; and various animals. In pondering the aforementioned juxtaposition, and reflecting on some of the past experiences of my own life in the streets, I reached the conclusion that we can be such idiots at times with the decisions that we make.

Let's look at a lion for example, world renowned as the king of the jungle. Even with it's enormous size, strength, and feared reputation, you will never catch a lion placing *himself* in a perilous situation. You will not catch him playing with, or showing a lack of respect for animals such as elephants and alligators because it knows that it has no win. In fact, if either of those animals are in close proximity, the lion will quickly vacate the premises. To do anything otherwise in a futile attempt to show bravery would be detrimental to it's survival, and it never risks it. Instead it sticks to the plan that was outlined for it, what I refer to as instinct, and usually lives it's life to the fullest. Whether the lion is "aware" of this plan or not is up for perennial discussion, but what we do know is that it will never intentionally put itself in harm's way.

Which brings the spotlight to us, preferably us street dudes. I am pretty sure that every one of us does not want to be in the proximity of a lion, but if you do, I tip my hat to you. With that said, why is it that we will consciously do the very thing that a lion would never do? Why would you intentionally throw yourself into a lifestyle that you know kills people on a daily basis, sometimes in bunches? Why would you take the chance of ending up like some of the dudes in your neighborhood, or even in your own family, who are locked up, just to impress people who really could care less about you?

I could go on and on with these type of questions, but you get the point. Each one reflects the end of the journey that you will make if you choose that path, nothing less. Can you really say that you love yourself, that you are taking care of yourself if you would be willing to knowingly put yourself in a position where the odds of getting hurt, or hurting someone else, are not in your favor? If things are bound to come full circle, isn't hurting someone else the equivalent of hurting yourself?

If you decided to sell drugs, knowing that it would kill your mother to see you locked up, and seeing her hurting would hurt you, why would you do it?

If you picked up a gun and decided to rob this kid because he has something that you want, do you think that he's going to go home and go about his normal routine? Do you not think that he's going to be plotting revenge against you, whether it's in the form of calling the police or resorting to the code of the streets (hit back harder)?

Any sane person who even halfway loved themselves wouldn't even be remotely interested in introducing that kind of drama into their life.

Self-realization. This brings everything to a head, and can even be placed first according to the person. Once you discover that you love yourself (truly), which means that you actually care what happens to you, then you will start to realize the things that you are doing to contradict that.

Are you treating this person, whether male or female; young or old; black, white, or any other nationality; gay or straight; like you want to be treated, with respect? You have to be comfortable enough with yourself to go against the grain of whatever is wrong, in order to do what you know is right. For young people these days, this is more about standing up and placing yourselves in the other person's shoes when you are tempted to do or say something harmful to someone, especially of your peer group. As we all know, this is called bullying. Over one million people commit suicide every year because they can't take the pain and embarrassment of being bullied, and this number is increasing. In knowing that you are an advocate for bullying, because that is exactly what you are if you don't stand against it, how does that make you feel? What if your differences were magnified on a daily basis, everywhere that you turned? Think about that. Just because someone is different from you doesn't mean that they are inferior, it doesn't mean that something is wrong with them, it's what makes them their own person. That is something that should be respected, not ridiculed, because it takes courage to be different.

Are you happy with yourself? Of course we can all improve ourselves, but that's not what I am talking about here. I'm talking about *you*, the essence of you, your imperfections, your values, your goals. Are you happy with all of that, because those things make you your own person?

Once you have successfully conquered those two questions, and incorporate them into the foundation of how you are going to structure your life, the remaining question is what are you going to do. If you really love and care about your life, you are going to take control of it, period. The fact of the matter is that everyone is going to end up somewhere later on down the line, that place depends solely on you. Regardless of if it's in a nice office working a good job, a rehabilitation center trying to overcome drug addiction, a penitentiary for trying to take the short cut to wealth, or a graveyard for the very same reason, it is inevitable.

Out of those choices, which one seems like the best, the nice office right?

If that was your choice, and I'm going to assume that it was, what are you doing to place yourself on that path? Though that may be where you want to end up, it's not just going to happen in the blink of an eye. There is still a long road ahead of you, one that is full of twists and turns in the form of temptation. One thing that we do know is that it all starts with you. You have to care enough, to love yourself enough, to want that happy ending for you and your loved ones. You have to be willing to make the sacrifices for it because it will come quickly, faster than you can even imagine if you start out on the wrong path.

I think that the first brother spelled it out completely for you, using his own mistakes as examples every step of the way. Though we can all see that he eventually arrived there mentally, I think that we are in agreement when we say that he would much rather have learned these things beforehand, when he could still embrace his family and help people far beyond the scope that being incarcerated will ever allow. He gave you the key components that will ultimately demonstrate your self-love, and keep you on the road to positive success:

1) Discipline
2) Direction
3) Accountability
4) Ambition
5) Basic Life Skills

These five things should also be a part of the foundation on which you begin to build your life, if you are striving for any type of positive success.

The second brother expressed the importance of sacrifice for a greater good. A line that stood out to me was: "Doing something with your life takes work, but truth be told, so does screwing it up." A hard head makes a soft you-know-what, so when people tell you that something is bad for you, no matter where they come from, stay away from it. Yeah you may lose a few cool points for it but trust me, you'll be giving them out once you start to reap the benefits from staying home to do that homework while others go out partying and all that it entails!

The third brother stressed the importance of knowing yourself. If there are things that you don't like about yourself that you can change, change them. If you can't, embrace them. Then you will be able to move forward and accept the fact that you are worthy of a productive future. Then you will discover the confidence needed for you to step out there and chase down any resource that you feel may be able to help you get to where you want to be.

The fourth brother shared his own issues with self-love, or the lack thereof, in his letter. He said that he had bought into the narrative of others that he couldn't be anything of value, so in turn he set out to live a de-valued life. How sadly profound is that? Is that how you are living right now? If so, do you see the end result of allowing others to determine and validate your existence?

You deserve any and every opportunity that is out there which can place you on the path toward living your dream, but until you understand and embrace that, no one else will either!

Chapter Four

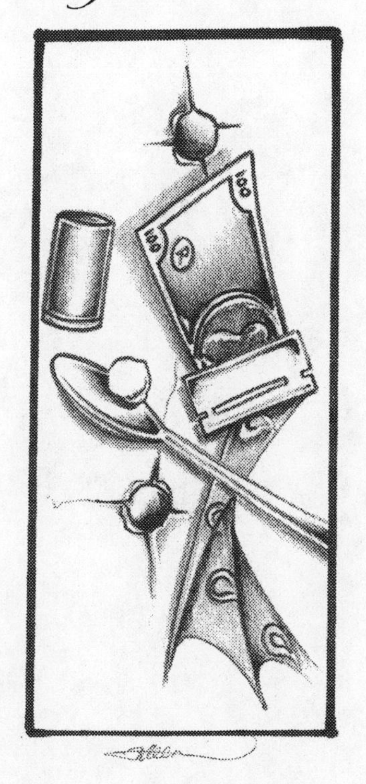

Surround yourself with what you seek.

From: Anonymous

What it wuz cuz! I start this off with this saying because for a long time, everything I did was based on this saying. I was a West Side Playboy Hustler's Crip Gang Member. At the time of this writing, I am thirty-three years old and on federal death row.

I'm writing this because hopefully my story can give you a bird's eye view of what can happen to you if you choose this lifestyle. Do you see how I said choose? Make no doubt about it, you do have a choice in the way you live your life.

Unlike a lot of dudes that you will read about, I am from a small town in Arkansas with about five thousand people living there. Like a lot of you, I was not raised by my parents, but by my grandparents. We were poor, but at the time I wasn't aware of it because we always had food and clean clothes, so it was all good to me until I got older.

My life changed in 1988 when my grandmother died of cancer. She was my rock, the one who made sure that I did my homework and obeyed. When she died, a lot of me died with her, but most importantly I had a couple of cousins who'd moved to town that was in the Crip gang. I looked up to them and the stories that they told made the gang life seem like the way to go. So, at the age of thirteen years old, I joined the West Side Playboy Hustler Crips. I started getting into trouble with the law and doing all the wrong things that my grandparents told me not to do, but when you're out there in the streets with your cuzzo, nothing matters but the "crippin'". I got into so much trouble that my grandparents sent me to live with my mother in Texas. Moving away from all of my homies was hard, but living with my mother was harder because she was not in my life that much. At that time I was full grown (15) and couldn't nobody tell me shit.

Texas was the beginning of the end for me.

It was like moving to the rich side of town, and everyone was into what I called "kid stuff", acting their age. I was into grown folk stuff, because I ran with people older than me. To make a long story short, I started selling drugs and getting money. Oh! I went to school everyday and was good at playing football, but my heart was in the streets.

After high school, I went to college for a year and even played semi-pro football, but once again, my heart was into the street life. Now, this is why I make a point to say that you have a choice.

Oh! I forgot to tell you that my mother got hooked on the same drug that I was selling. After she got hooked on crack and I almost put my hands on her for stealing my drugs, that made me stop selling crack and move to weed.

Now is the time that we look at what got me here on death row. I was charged with murder and running a "CCE" (Continuing Criminal Enterprise) or drug gang, working in six states. At the age of twenty-two, I owned a clothing store and a CD store. I had already had many of your favorite rappers in concert, and went to many cities across the country doing my so called ballin' thing. What I'm telling you now is to let you know where I've been, not to glorify any of it. What's so bad about many of us locked up is that we could have made better choices, but instead we went with the universal lie, believing that the choices that we made were the only ones we had coming from the hood. I pray that ya'll get something out of my story and make better choices.

I must end this story with the changes that I have made since the inception of my incarceration. I have given my life to Christ as my Lord and savior. I have changed my life around and you don't know how hard this was for me to put on paper because it was me talking about the old me.

Before I go, I want everyone to think about this: Everyone says that the hood only has bad things to offer like drugs and the game. If that was the case, then why is not everyone in the hood locked up? What about the person that picks up the trash, or the one that works at the corner store, or the one who cuts your hair? Just put that on your brain, then you can start to see through all of the bullshit that the streets are selling.

Much Respect,
June 7, 2010

From: Anonymous

When I was young my moms frequently told me that everyone has a story to tell. I used to think it was funny, or that it was some type of joke. As I got older and wiser, I started to go through life's experiences and I realized what my mom really meant.

They say that the best teacher is experience. That's why we as humans always pass our stories on to the next, so that hopefully our youth won't make the same mistakes that we made. There is no doubt that we all make mistakes, the most important thing is to not make the same mistake repeatedly.

You shouldn't even have to wonder why so many people stress the importance of getting your education. Education helps us for our future, it prepares us to become whatever we want to be in life. A person once asked me, "How could school be so hard when you have a teacher and a book teaching you the work?" Just think about that. No one said anything about it being easy, what in life is? We can achieve anything in life, but it starts with an education.

We all have someone that we look up to in one way or another. It can be our parents, a relative, or even a celebrity. You can believe that it was a struggle for them to get where they are today, even if it's not where they want to be in life. The struggle is what makes us who we are.

A relationship can affect us in many ways such as physically, mentally, and emotionally. We start to notice relationships in our households with our parents. Some see our parents in an abusive relationship and start to become accustomed to it, creating the false notion that it is okay to keep accepting a person back into a relationship that is abusive. Also, some women have the idea that having a baby will help them keep a man. Having a child changes everything. As kids, we always say that we can't wait until we get older, not knowing about all of the responsibilities that come with being an adult.

Most people believe that choosing the streets is an easy way to make it life. I'm here to tell you that it requires selfish dedication. The drug game has so many twists to it, it's not even funny. Yeah at first we all set our goals, thinking that we're going to make a certain amount of money and get out. But once we get in, one goal leads to another, and with more money comes problems. You see, nobody tells you that a whole lot of problems come with the game because they don't want you to lose interest. Misery loves company! There's only two ways out of this, and that's death or jail, nothing in between.

Life is a struggle and there's no easy way around it!!! We all have life experiences one way or another, you have to keep striving to overcome all obstacles. Peace.

March 25, 2010

From: Anonymous

I really don't know how to start off this message other than if you've read up to this point then you must be on the road to redemption and one step closer to being able to assist someone in completing a similar transition off of a path of failure, tragedy, misery, and loneliness; and onto the road of happiness, success, and freedom. Please heed my advice, it could save your life, or save you from having to make the mistake of taking the life of another.

I'll start off by saying that I'm a twenty-seven year old Hispanic from Palm Beach County, Florida, which within the last decade has once been the murder capitol, cocaine capitol, and some more shit. The chances of failure were great, but there were also chances for success. Some of the best NFL players came from my county such as Santonio Holmes (NY Jets), Fred Taylor (N.E), and Devin Hester (Chi). These are some of the guys that rose above the negativity.

Now let me tell you that I was drawn to the streets due to watching my uncle rise in the game, instilling fear in people through violence and manipulation as a gang member, pimp, and smooth talker. I witnessed his work at twelve years old and ever since then, I became him.

I joined the Maniac Latin Disciples at age fourteen, but I had been under their influence since I was thirteen. The older guys were who I wanted to be like and impress, but in the end they all turned out to be either rats or baseheads. I remember the old coons around the hood always telling me: "Damn youngin your record is still juvenile, go to school, get a job, and stop being the dude in the desert." Being in the desert was a term used in my hood, it translated to describe the mindstates of dudes in the streets. People in the desert are always seeing mirages and chasing them, so the term was really an amalgamation of a metaphor and an analogy. I was chasing something that was at home all along, love.

I'm about to be twenty-eight in four months, and I have eleven years in prison. No kids, no wife. Somehow I managed to get two death sentences, five life sentences, eighty-five years, and charges pending in other counties and states.

Please don't be another statistic, because one misstep affects a whole race. For example, once you get a felony you can't vote, and on what I believe to be a much larger scale, you can't get jury duty. If you can't get jury duty, you can't accurately assist someone's legal situation, leaving them vulnerable to individuals who cannot understand the reasoning or culture behind committing crimes. This translates to people like you, getting biased juries that will slam you for something that they can't even fathom.

So listen to them aunts, uncles, your parents, and whoever else is trying to tell you something good. In the end, they are the ones who will assist you in court as a witness, or be the ones who write you and send you money to make it. Felons can't visit, so basically the people that you're dissin' your family for, won't even be able to help you anyway.

If you take anything away from this, JUST STAY UP OUT THEM STREETS!

February 20, 2011

Positive Surroundings

You are who you hang with, plain and simple. As much as we all like to make a conscious effort to maintain our own individuality, this is the unfortunate truth. Think about it, have you ever saw a group of police officers huddled in a crowd and assumed that one of them was a dentist? Of course not. If you are hanging around cops, than it is most likely that you either are one, or want to be one someday.

Another way to look at things is by evaluating all of your relationships using just one question: Is this person either helping me, or hurting me? When it boils down to it, those are the only two types of people that exist. It's not about looking for something in return or establishing relationships for personal gain, this is just black-and-white truth.

Remember when I spoke about the importance of positive perception? Well that is not restricted to just you. You also have to be conscious of the positions that you place yourself in not only for people to perceive you as a positive person, but for them to *treat* you as such also. Being as though progress is built on the shoulders of good relationships, this is key. Richard Parsons, once the CEO of Time Warner, once said something that attested to this very point in my opinion. When asked how he had managed to rise to the top of a Fortune 500 company, despite growing up in one of the roughest neighborhoods in Brooklyn, New York, he simply stated: "If you want to go fast, go alone; if you want to go far, go with others."

As much as we like to tell ourselves that we don't care what other people think, is that really true? Of course no one should have the power to steal your happiness, but if you are not viewed in a positive light, who in their right mind is going to want to jeopardize their success for you? Subsequently, what doors are going to open?

In case you didn't know, the answer to the first question is nobody, and the answer to the second one is none.

This point can also be flipped and viewed from the other end of the spectrum that we have been focusing on throughout this book, the underworld or, the streets.

In order to be accepted and respected in that lifestyle, do you think that you have to have a 2.0 grade point average? Do you have to have a library card in order to stand on a corner and sell drugs, or wait behind a wall so that you can get the drop on an unsuspecting victim? Nope.

All that is required is that you be able to disengage yourself from your foundation as a human being, your humanity. Now this may sound like it's not much, or that it's easy, but when you hit rock bottom and actually get a chance to look back you will see things differently.

You have to be able to totally disregard the feeling that you would get if you caught someone selling crack cocaine to your mother, in order to repeatedly step into their house and sell some to their's.

You have to be able to ignore the anger that you would feel if you were to get robbed for something that may have sentimental value, in order to be able to rob the next person.

You have to be able, and willing, to say the hell with your mother or father, or both, because that is what your actions will scream while they are constantly pleading for you to do something different, to no avail.

You have to be willing and able to *kill* someone, to physically remove another mother's child from this earth, because at some point you will be tested. No one is going to fully respect you out there until they are made aware of the consequences for not doing so. Once that starts, it's either kill or be killed because you are now in the big leagues, a membership that will stay with you forever. The majority of the people that you will encounter, will be functioning on the exact same wave length that you are required to, thus spawning competition, and you know that it is only a matter of time until things get way out of hand for the weak.

If you can't meet any of these requirements, and be thankful if you don't, then no doors are going to open for you in the streets. The ones that will open, won't be a gateway that will lead you to making any real money, because that will attract the very wolves that we just described.

Can you imagine that? Who wants to live like that everyday? Before you answer yourself, please know that I didn't even begin to scratch the surface in describing some of the people that you will cross paths with out there.

Now I don't know about you, but going to school and setting up the building blocks for you to make legit money, and building solid, trustworthy relationships sounds like the better move. In order for you to do that though, you have to be aware of the company that you keep. Scratch that, you don't have to, other people will do that for you, and make the necessary preparations when they see you coming.

Is that right, the fact that we live in a judgemental world? Probably not, but it's life.

If you are an aspiring basketball player, or doctor, don't get upset when people start to cut their eyes at you because they constantly see you hanging on the corner with drug dealers. You are who you hang with, or you want to be someday.

If you want to do something legit and build a sustainable life for yourself, surround yourself with people that you know have the same agenda. This is applying direction to your ambition because ambition without direction can land you in positions where the decision required could cost you your life. Surrounding yourself with positive people will also put you in a position to build solid contacts for the latter part of your life early on, not to mention potentially save you from catching a bullet or two, or ten.

Those of you who are in inner city environments where the majority of your friends are already entrenched in the streets, you have a decision to make.

You can either maintain the individuality that you say that you want by sticking to your guns and following the path that will safely lead you to your dream; or you can succumb to the pressures of trying to fit in, and head down a path that is much more perilous in the name of friendship. Have you ever heard the street adage: You don't have to be in jail to be doing time? Well that is very true under many circumstances. In this instance, you can be imprisoned in narrow visions of friendship and manhood.

Making the choice to follow your dream the right way does not mean that you don't have love for your friends anymore, it just shows that you love yourself enough to entertain a future. It also doesn't mean that you've turned your back on them either. There comes a time when you have to start noticing people for exactly who they are. If they are really your friends first of all, they will respect your decision. Real friends always want to see their buddies get ahead, no matter what avenues they may choose.

The second thing that you need to realize is that you can't be of help to anyone if you don't have yourself in order. We have continuously revisited this issue throughout this book because of it's importance. If your primary excuse for hanging with them is that you want to have their backs, then you can still have their backs when you achieve some success in your field. This will make you much more effective because you will be able to offer a helping hand in the form of a job referral, or just sheer proof that success is attainable with a little hard work and dedication.

Once you find yourself in such a position, then you can really see who wants better for *themselves*, and who is just happy with hurting people while slowly destroying themselves in the process. Real people always want to do better, and they never let an opportunity to get out of a negative situation slip by. If you extend your hand from a positive perspective and they don't take it, then they never meant well to begin with. They were simply crabs in a barrel, constantly clawing and grabbing at you in an effort to keep you from breaking out so that you could reach your highest potential.

As you can see from the first brother's letter, everything was fine as long as he was in the right company. It wasn't until his grandmother died (may she rest in peace), and his cousins introduced him to the Crip lifestyle, that his life began to spiral out of control. She didn't know him as Scarface, only Julius, the grandson that she had high expectations for, and made conscious efforts to put her best foot forward to set good examples to follow. Once he began to encounter people who were on the wrong path themselves, they joined hands and the rest is history, now his-story that is used to show the importance of your surroundings. He didn't have to do some of the things that he did, and neither do you. If he had the chance now, he emphatically expressed how different things would be. Unfortunately he doesn't have that chance at the moment, but you do.

In the words of the second brother: "Nobody tells you that a whole lot of problems come with the game, because they don't want you to lose interest." Think about that.

The third brother gave you a few examples of people that rose from the ashes of his very neighborhood because they made the right decisions. The people that he named happened to have atheletic talent, but I'm sure that there are countless others that also made it out to do something different, something that they dreamed of doing. They chose not to do what he wanted to do, and now their lives couldn't be more different.

If I told you that if you stepped out of your house at two o'clock on the dot today, someone was going to shoot you dead right on your front porch, would you go outside at that exact time? If you're smart, no!

Well this is no different. You have written proof in your hands right now, telling you what will happen if you continue to run with the wrong people, people that are in direct contradiction to what you want to achieve and who you want to be. We are living out the consequences for having done what you are either thinking about doing, or are currently doing.

Do you still want to live like that?

Chapter Five

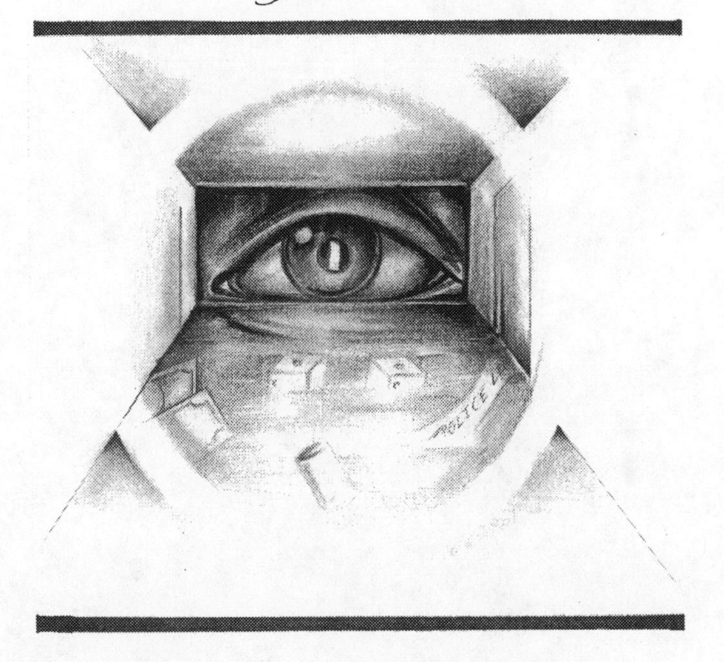

Nobody can do you better than you can.

From: Anonymous

You remind me so much of myself when I was your age. I was just like you, or should I say, you are just like me. Growing up, I would always make decisions that would put me in the position of a follower instead of a leader. That would have been okay if I was following the more positive type of people instead of those who sold drugs all day, did drugs, carried guns, and other things that were self-destructive and along the lines of living the street life. These were the kind of people that I dealt with everyday, spent most of my time with, and developed a certain type of admiration for, wanting to mimic what I saw in them. I mean hey, why not? They wore nice clothes, had lots of money, a lot of people respected them, they all hung out late, and they seemed popular. Little did I know that with these type of people, trouble wasn't far behind. Little did I know that living that type of lifestyle came with a price. A price that I did not know I would have to pay, they would all eventually pay, in which the currency would be my life and/or my freedom. I looked up to these people, when they taught me absolutely nothing. I showed so much love for these people at a young age (About the same as you are right now), and thought them all to be my friends. Real friends would have pointed me in a different direction. I say all that to say that I know you look up to me, and want to live the same lifestyle I lived when I was growing up. I don't want to be responsible for inspiring you to be like the old me because what you are attracted to within me, I am no longer attracted to, nor am I conducting myself as the character you fell in love with. Please allow me to share with you a little bit of what my life was like when I was around your age . . .

I was very energetic, excited, and full of life when I was a young man. I remember when people at school would ask me what

I wanted to be when I got older. I would reply by saying that I wanted to be a police officer or a singer. Now I was able to hold a note a little bit, or better yet, I was okay at harmonizing whenever I was in the shower (laughs). However, singing in the shower just won't cut it in the music world. I wanted to be a police officer so that I could help stop some of the crime that overwhelmed my neighborhood.

I always loved school and became interested in sports early on. I was really good in football and loved to play the position of running back. I used to be so small and fast at the same time that I was hard to catch! I was very good at playing basketball as well. I was actually better at that, it soon became my favorite sport. Just the feeling that would run through my body when I had the ball in my hand and knew that the team was relying on me! I would come down the court dribbling the ball thinking to myself "We gonna win, can't nobody stop me, I see the weakness in their defense already, I got 'em, I got 'em, I got 'em", and as soon as I got down the court I would either pick their defense apart with my dribbling and penetration skills, or I would pull up and shoot the ball. In my mind I would have already made it because I had so much confidence in myself. Majority of the time, I would make the shot and then yell at the top of my lungs, "Let's go back, they can't stop me!", as I would run back down towards the other end of the court, beating my chest with a closed fist to add emphasis on everything I spoke. Those were days. Those were some of the best times of my life, and I was so happy with myself, my game, my talent, and the world in general (I was a kid).

As time went by, I stopped wanting to be a singer and wanted to play in the NBA one day or be a police officer. I always loved to attend school, and still to this day think about how fun school was at times. It was a place to interact with others, make friends, develop bonds with teachers, learn things that will help you throughout life, and to share what you'd learned by helping other students with their work. Finishing my work fast, and being able to recite what I'd learned in school for my parents was a really good feeling to me. Like I said before, I was a kid. I used to love to stand in front of the class and do presentations on the topic of discussion in school for the day. In time, I stopped wanting to be a police officer and started to want to be a lawyer and play in the NBA. To become a lawyer, I knew I had to complete school. Even though I loved playing basketball, and wanted to be a lawyer, I was becoming more and more involved with the guys in my neighborhood. That's where I picked up the nasty habit of smoking. It began with cigarettes, then weed, and soon it was PCP and liquor.

I can honestly tell you now that drugs are not the way if you have any dreams at all of being successful in life. Even though the weed smoke and PCP was making me feel good, and smoking period made me look like a perfect piece to the puzzle of the in-crowd, it was unknown to me that I was losing all focus of becoming a lawyer, and whenever I would play basketball I would be so high or out of wind (due to the smoke damaging my lungs) that I couldn't perform like I usually would. This continued every time I played until I eventually just gave up all together. At one point I wanted to give up school too, but my mother was there to help me. I loved her so much that I wouldn't stop going. Subsequently, I ended up graduating from high school, receiving my diploma. I was always intelligent, just like you are, but my downfall was that I chose the wrong company, just like you are doing right now. I gradually started to invest my time into what they were doing. In time, the thought of playing basketball professionally, and being a lawyer, wouldn't even cross my mind any more. All I wanted to do was smoke weed, stay out late, and smoke some more with the fellas, all along wasting my time and my childhood.

If you remember, a few times in the midst of this letter I would stop and say that (I was a kid).

When I was living as a kid, being a kid, and enjoying life as a kid should, those were some of the best times of my life. Three months after my graduation I was locked up, and now I'm writing to you from a prison cell. I know right, my life story seems short doesn't it? That's because at the young age of 18, I was locked up for an incident stemming from the crowd I hung around and sentenced to twenty years in prison. That's two years longer than my overall age was at the time! It was my time and turn to pay. If you remember towards the beginning of this letter I said that "Living this type of lifestyle came with a price that we would all have to pay." Well, those very same guys that I looked up to and followed, are all currently in prison as well with sentences ranging from fifteen years all the way up to life without parole, both state and federal time. I looked up to, admired, and ended up following them right into prison. Even though I didn't want to be that involved in the in-crowd that it would land me in prison, it's all apart of the outcome when you are living the kind of lifestyle that you are currently attracted to, that I and so many others inadvertently inspired in you. Either this or death.

If I knew then what I know now, I would have stuck with trying to be like Allen Iverson, Michael Jordan, or Kobe Bryant. I mean why not? They wear the best clothes, have lots of money, everyone respects and loves them, and they are so very popular. And, it doesn't cost them their freedom or their life. Don't risk your life or freedom trying to be anything like I was or trying to chase the lifestyle that I was living. I'm telling you now, it ain't worth it! I've been locked up since I was 18 years old and I'm now 27. I don't want you to go through that and neither should you. Go to school, stay focused, and grow up to be somebody. Hey, maybe I can be more inspired by you.

September 14, 2010

From: Anonymous

me vs ME
(my lower self) vs (MY HIGHER SELF)

I wasn't satisfied with being free. (Following the laws put in place by society, being able to make "my own choices", moving around freely without being told what to do, or taking advantage of the fortuities which came my way).

Instead, i chose to say "Fuck it, I'm going to do shit my way!" That's the truth. No cut, no bullshit! Now due to the choices I made, and the mentality I had at the time, I find myself in what I like to call, "The Nigga's Retirement Home."

I'm in prison! Not only that, I'm on federal death row! But the worst part of it all is that there's a chance that I could be executed behind some bullshit that's beneath me . . .

I could make every "excuse" in the book about why I'm in prison. I could give you countless would've, could've, should've's. Instead, I chose to keep it 100 and say that I was too much of a coward to be the man I knew I could be. (The man who I am now.)

All of us have been given the free will to make choices which will help determine which direction our lives will go. Some of us might be better off than others, whether that's financially, physically, etc., but in the end we all have a choice.

I grew up in St. Louis, Missouri. I grew up in the part of the city, which was not only known for getting money, but the part of the city which took pride in the amount of bodies it could pile up. (To those who lived there, it was called: The Cemetary.)

I lived in a single parent home. We weren't the brokest family on the block, but we weren't the richest either. We didn't have much at home, but we got by with what we had.

While we didn't have much, one thing I did have was a mother who stressed the importance of a good education. She told me the benefits of securing one, and what could happen if I didn't. But like the old saying goes: "You can lead a horse to water, but you can't make it drink."

To try to keep me from being killed or going to prison, my mother enrolled me into a school that was not only far away from the city, but the kids who went there came from some of St. Louis' most elite families. (She took advantage of the voucher program.)

I'd ride the bus to school, whereas the kids who I'd go to class with, their parents dropped them off in Cadillacs, Benz's, etc. I'm talking about cars we'd see on television or in magazines and be like, "That's my car!"

I'd bring in lunch meat, an apple, and some penny candy for lunch. The other kids would bring in five-star meals that their home chefs hooked up for them. They also wore top of the line clothes, and I was probably wearing the cloths that they'd donated to the Goodwill.

My mother didn't care about the things that the other kids had that I didn't. She felt that the playing field was even because my education mirrored theirs. She would always echo that line from The Fresh Prince: Parents just don't understand. She'd say, "Boy, go to school to learn, not for a fashion show."

What she said was real talk at the time, but I wanted to tell her to wear what I had to wear and then we could talk. (But knowing how confident my mother was in herself, she would've worn the clothes and been proud of it.)

Me though, (to be honest) for a little while, I felt uncomfortable as hell. But I never showed it. See, I didn't have low self esteem or anything like that. When you're put in a position that's new to you, you just have to find your footing.

I had something that was rare for most kids who grew up where I came from and was looked down on by the majority of the kids around them. I had charisma and swag.

These two qualities would change the opinions of most of the kids. I knew that I had "something" inside of me, and I had no problem letting that be known.

I was from "the hood", but I wasn't a fool. I did my homework (for a period of time), I played sports, and I was in with the (in-crowd). When I was in school, I felt like I was in another world . . . but whenever the school bell rang at three-thirty, and it was time to go home, I went back into survival mode.

I went to school in the suburbs, but I ate, slept, and lived in the jungle. I felt like I was living two lives. I found myself dumbing down when I'd be around "my homies". I say that because while I could've used my education to better my life, I applied what I learned in school to the streets.

It wasn't like I could talk to the people I hung out with about what I learned in school, as far as education was concerned, I was at least two grades ahead of everyone I knew . . . . So I dealt with people on their level. (But if I saw that you wanted to grow, then I'd build with you.)

The way that I'd use my mind on the streets would attract the attention of some of the cities most powerful hustlers and gangsters. (That way of life wasn't new to me because some of my family members were deep into the game.)

For a few years, the mental battle between me and ME would go on. Let's just say that by the time I was sixteen, I'd won the top art prize at school, I'd made a name for myself on the streets as a "hustler", and I went to jail.

Believe me, I wanted to do good all the time! But when one of my friends was killed, I did what most "niggaz" do. I made an "excuse" as to why I couldn't do the right thing, and I took the "easy" way out. (me had won).

I ended up leaving the elite school so that I could be around my friends in the city school, "the real" people. That's when I saw why I was two grades ahead of most people.

The education system was the worst. The books were not only limited, but they were for kids in a lower grade level. Then the teachers (some), didn't even care. We'd skip classes, go smoke weed, and the times I chose not to go to school, I'd grind!

I could out hustle any ten people you put against me. I had a squad of four, and we ran things like a business. I had a choice to make between school and hustling, and school lost. I put my all into the game, but no matter how much money I made, no matter how many women I had, and no matter how high I got, REAL TALK, I felt empty. See, when everything was gone and I had to face me, I knew I was better than how I was living . . .

I was blessed with a lot of talent. I could draw, paint, write, play sports, and I always had a way of seeing an opportunity in every situation. The worst part about all of this is not having someone who could nourish, and help me further these things.

My mother's education went as far as a GED. But her work ethic was A-1. Most people in my family, their education didn't go as far as high school. So how could they nourish or help further talents they knew nothing about?

In the hood, we want things quick. We see "white people" with luxury cars, nice clothes, and big houses, and we want those things too. Yes, some were born into money. But we fail to see the underlying picture . . . they "worked" for it! We have the pressures of fitting in, not getting shot, stabbed, jumped, and/or harassed by the police. We begin to program our minds to think that that's all we are worth.

See, I knew that I could do great things, but I just didn't know what, or how I was going to get there . . . so i shrunk down to my lower self and took the same way out that most weak people take. I abandoned the ME that I knew I could be, and settled for the me who didn't require much effort to establish.

I allowed what the streets thought about me to play on the fact that I wasn't sure who I wanted to be. Who wants to be a square, a nerd, or any of the names affiliated with being smart? I didn't want to at the time. I chose to luxuriate in my ignorance of what it was like not to be a MAN.

I think that that's why I didn't find pleasure in the game that some found, because any unknowledgeable person with a little percipience to do wrong could get in the game.

I let down everyone who really loved me. I put my loyalty for the streets before my loyalty to my family, and most of all, my mother. By being the person she taught me not to be, I was disrespecting "everything" about her. I might as well have said she wasn't shit, because i ignored her love, her advice, and her guidance. If I wasn't going to live my life for ME, then I should have lived for her.

When I look back at my life, I see that I had chances to make something of myself. Forget about the elite school I went to. I should've took advantage of the education they tried to offer me in the city school. So what they were behind. My dumb ass wasn't smart enough to put myself ahead. I wouldn't have had the best education, but at least I could have secured one.

If I would've put half of the energy into doing right as I did into doing wrong, there's no limit to what I could've done. But, while I didn't take advantage of bettering myself when I was out, I wasn't going to lay down because I was in prison.

I sat back one day and introduced me to ME, and when I was able to see me in so many others who I encountered, I knew I had to change. Who wants to be a dumb nigga "all" their life? There comes a time when you have to become a MAN, and realize that you don't have to live down to your lower self just to fit in, or be "loved" by your homies. No matter if you're hustling or if you're doing right, "niggas" are going to hate you. Weak niggas want to hold you back and keep you from doing right, because they are too weak to be dumb on their own. I say, "Fuck them."

Now, I'm the owner of my own company. I stay away from "all" things that are negative! It's hard because of where I come from, but what makes it easy is I got tired of being me.

Why wait until later to become the MAN or WOMAN that you can become now? If you need help bettering yourself, get at me! (Just mention that you read one of G's books)!

CEO of MEHZMERIZED L.L.C.
July 10, 2010

Name: Anonymous

Hey G, I really appreciate you involving my life in this project that you're doing. Even though I know that I somewhat delayed your process, I want you to understand that I was somewhat apprehensive. That was totally on my end because I didn't know how far I would go in terms of expressing my emotions. But when I saw how much you put into this project, it hurt me because I felt like I had let you down. So I had to man up.

See I feared being lost in life due to anxiety and many self-doubts; from peer pressure about my lack of education, mainly in reading. You know, when kids are in class and everybody starts to laugh once they discover that you can't read the basic words. I found that my personality helped me with teachers to pass me on, but at the same time it hurt me because academically outside of math, I was lost in every sense.

I really couldn't understand it because all of my other siblings were very smart academically. It wasn't like I wasn't trying. I was as eager as everyone else, and I put a lot into it. See I have the greatest mother in the world, hands down. She would come home from work, cook, and then go sell her Avon stuff so that she would have extra money to support us all. With all of this on her shoulders as a single mother, she would still take the time to help me with my reading. To this day, our relationship is as tight as a piece of thread trying to get through the smallest needle hole. She always put so much into me, and I felt like I let her down when it came to my reading. That's what kept me trying; her. But I have to be truthful, the pressure of other kids in class seeing me studder as I struggled to read, was too much for a fourth grader to handle.

One quality that was very much evident in my character through all of my struggles early on, was my leadership. Even at an early age, I could organize kids to pass out the neighborhood grocery store flyers and pay them accordingly. I had relationships with many of the store owners in my neighborhood because of the returns on the bottles that I hustled. Then, when other kids would beat me to the flyer distribution job, it would involve repercussions of violence because I felt that was my territory. The only way I would let them get out of fighting me, was to join my team. I couldn't read in school, but I was unbelievable in math. That quality was perfect for my street endeavors because I refused to take shorts in my business deals. I guess the hustle in me was a direct gift from my mother.

I found comfort in the streets as time progressed. I totally accepted it because it never allowed my doubts to surface. Being that reading wasn't my strong suit, it wasn't needed for me to survive in the violent jungle that was known as the Chicago street life. I excelled in that arena, so much so that I managed to garner a huge spotlight, much like the kids who made the honor roll in school.

As I look back in retrospect, all of the attention acquired from the platform that I had built for myself, became an addiction. Now it's not about glorifying any of this, but I'd be lying to you if I said that I didn't find pleasure in my importance in the community. I guess you could say that I became the principle of the school of hard knocks, the only difference was that this principle carried a big gun and his finger was super quick to pull the trigger. School in the traditional sense was now non-existent, it was all about the streets and maintaining my reputation both in and outside of my community. This mindstate would eventually propel me into the upper echelon of the Gangster Disciples, making me a board member.

Little did I know that this same mindstate would eventually take me and sixty-eight others to the federal penitentiary. Wanting to stand out back then would spiral way out of control later because out of the sixty-eight, I would be the only one to land on death row.

Do you remember in the beginning when I said that I tried my hardest for my mother? Well as time progressed, I would eventually have another love in my life, my daughter. I also have a host of nieces and nephews that are like my children as well.

As I entered what would be the second phase of my life, prison, these very people would serve as the impetus for my change of mind. Sitting on death row, I was forced to think. I began to look back on all of the lives that were lost on my journey to this point, how I could have used my leadership to help build things in my community, instead of destroy them. I could have easily influenced those around me to become successful the right way, instead of the way that we chose. Now as I lay here somedays with tears in my eyes, I think of their children, a generation much like some of you, that have to grow up without their fathers. Now their mothers have to play two roles, just like my mother did when I was growing up.

One of the biggest things that I have come to realize is that I could have been just as successful with my reading and everything else, if I had only stuck it out.

After coming to grips with my wrongs and taking the time to conquer my demons, I began a spiritual journey that would eventually lead me to Islam. It brought about so many things within me, humbleness, purity, compassion, caring. It made me an overall better human being.

Now my mission is to be a positive inspiration for kids like you, using my past as your guide. I tell my kids today that it takes more strength to do what's right than what's wrong. The same peer pressure that I felt in the fourth grade so long ago, I use as an example to tell them not to worry about what people say. It's all about putting your best foot forward, ensuring that you will be able to make a positive choice whenever faced with adversity. That keeping it real shit, that's for the birds! Keeping it real is being there for your family when they need you, being able to put smiles on their faces because you've done something that they can brag about, not be ashamed of.

Today, my mother runs a day care center for children in the community. My daughter attends college. My nieces and nephews attend college, and the others attend high school. It makes me proud to see that they take pride in getting good grades.

As for myself, I write books, movie scripts, and I look forward to other business endeavors that will hopefully inspire young people out there to do the right thing. It is my ultimate goal to establish the Pop's Foundation, helping kids conquer self-esteem issues, learn about computers for the world of tomorrow, art, music, and effective writing. Praise Allah!

March 2, 2011

Tunnel Vision

I always like to use the thought of a long road as a metaphor for life. Though some of you may not exactly want to admit it, being able to drive is a skill that has to be taught and cultivated over time. You are not born knowing how to drive, just as you are not born with the blueprint of your life already etched in your mind. You have to take baby steps in order to develop that skill so that you will not only be a safe driver, but a trustworthy one as well.

For driving in the literal sense, baby steps come in the form of enrolling in driver's education classes, followed by obtaining your learner's permit, followed by taking the test that will actually prove that you have what it takes to drive alone, without supervision. These are the things that will prepare you for when you actually get out onto that busy road or highway, surrounded by others who have their own agenda as you begin to navigate your way to your desired destination.

Now if you're driving on the road of life, things can be a little more complicated. This process also requires baby steps, and hopefully I have done a good job of highlighting each one in each of the previous chapters.

A quick recap shows that everything starts with a positive outlook. When you think positive, you increase the chances of positive things happening in your life. Even if your surroundings are not the best, when you take the time to stop and tell yourself that there is a better way, you are placing yourself on a productive path. This shows that you are not content with just going with the flow of what you perceive to be a negative situation.

Once you have your thoughts in order you are well on your way because you have discovered that you have a role to play in your own life, which will determine how it ultimately turns out. Simply stated, you have a purpose. Once this is realized, you can actually start to sit down and evaluate different avenues on which you will build the foundation of your life. Building on the proper foundation, as we have discussed, is perhaps the most important part of this process because it will determine your overall outcome. If your foundation is crooked or cracked, everything that you build on top of it will crumble in due time. If you decide to make drug dealing your foundation, acquiring the quick dollar, then everything as a result of that is automatically in peril. Things may not go wrong immediately or all at once, but they will go wrong nonetheless. If you decide that you want to go to school and prepare for a future, bypassing all of the headaches that will inevitably come with hanging in the streets, you will have laid a foundation that will never be able to be destroyed or taken away from you.

Discovering your purpose will undoubtedly spark a sense of self-love inside of you that is very much lucid. This self-love will be on display for all to see, both good and bad people, and will release you from the self-imposed stress of allowing others to dictate your worth to you. That love should give you the strength to buckle down and go for whatever it is that you desire in life with an undying passion, regardless of the profession that you choose.

Next comes what I think is the obvious, the company that you keep. Though we have established that everyone is unique in their own right, that does not mean that everyone is compatible at any given moment. If you have made the conscious decision to do something with your life, you should not be able to look inside of your personal circle and see people who have chosen to let their's spiral out of control. It doesn't matter what their relation is to you, how long you have known them, or how cool they may seem, their actions should always be up for evaluation. Either they are helping or hurting remember? These are the only two types of people that you are going to encounter as you navigate your way through life, there is no in-between. If you are determined to do the right thing in hopes of building a successful career and having a happy life, you should not have people around you who you *know* are doing things that threaten those aspirations. They will only distract you, thus hindering the process of you reaching your full potential.

Once you have realized the importance of, and applied each of the steps outlined in the previous chapters to your life, there is only one thing left to do. This final component may prove to be the most difficult, but difficult is not impossible. You must keep your eyes and actions trained on your goal, blocking everything detrimental out as you maintain your efforts to move toward it. This is known as tunnel vision to some, but widely recognized as focus. Focus is a skill that has to be cultivated, and to do so requires a tremendous amount of discipline. With it you will be able to not only attain whatever it is that you may desire, but also sustain the fruits of your labor.

Going back to the metaphor that we started with at the beginning of this chapter. Once you have adequately prepared yourself for the long road of life, you will have to actually get out there and hold your own amongst other drivers. Much like yourself, these other drivers will have also taken baby steps in an effort to prepare for the opportunity, but not all of them will have decided to take those steps in the right direction. Some of them will have impaired vision due to the way that they have perceived things up to that moment. Subsequently, the manner in which they will be managing their vehicles will pose a threat to the lane that you have created for yourself. This is one of the many scenarios that will test your focus.

There will also be bystanders on your journey, some of which won't qualify as innocent. They will be standing on the side, stagnant in their own lives, trying to persuade you to stop and kick it with them or either let them join you. They may not always be malicious, or easy to recognize behind their smiles and kind words. In fact, some of them might even be genuinely nice people. But if they are doing things which they are unaware of that you recognize as being hazardous to what it is that you are trying to accomplish, that makes them twice as dangerous.

In an effort to stay in line with the brothers in this chapter, I want to touch on the importance of maintaining your focus in a place where most of us tend to go astray, school. Education is the most powerful weapon that you can possess, at this point I trust that at the very least, their is a common consensus on that. With that said, it can and will be hard to keep that etched in your mind as you press forward while constantly being tempted by the many things that have the power to destroy your life. The guys with money and cars that you see on your way to and from school everyday; the popularity contest that seems to take center stage *in* school on a daily basis, and what it will take in order to be able to compete; bullies, for the unfortunate; the feelings of inferiority that you may get when you find yourself comparing your scholastic productivity to that of your peers; the turning to drugs for either recreation, or a defense mechanism that protects you from the pain of having to deal with the day to day stress of being in one of the aforementioned positions; the list goes on and on.

These are just a fraction of the myriad number of things that so frequently cause our young people to lose focus in what should be regarded as the most important place of their lives, school. As a result of this, they tend to fall behind so far that many of them opt to just give up and try a different route, one that has a dead end.

Statistics show that seventy-five percent of state inmates are school dropouts, as well as fifty-nine percent of federal inmates. They also show that students from low-income families have a ten percent dropout rate, and that dropouts are three-and-a-half times more likely to be incarcerated than those who graduate.

Whether you are a parent, or a young person experiencing tough times in school, those numbers should inspire some thought. It is essential that you not only believe that you are worthy of an education, no matter who you are, and that you maintain your focus while in pursuit of it and everything thereafter. The brothers in this chapter each gave you accounts of their battles with maintaining their focus, and shared the consequences that you can expect if you lose it.

The first brother almost lost his during his high school years due to drugs and living the street life, but with the love and support of his loving mother managed to make it through. Sadly, things went downhill shortly after his graduation as a result of the habits that he'd picked up, which is a testament to the fact that focus is something that is on-going. Even after school, you must keep your eyes on the prize when in the midst of temptation. Had he maintained the same perspective off the court as he did whenever he was on it, I'm confident that he would have been sharing his hard-earned wisdom with you face to face from a much different position.

The second brother gave you what I believe to be an excellent example. He compared his lower self (me), to his higher self (ME). Knowing the importance of getting an education, largely due to his mother, he set out to do the right thing. It wasn't until he took his eye off the prize that he started to notice things that were virtually non-existent before. The clothes that he wore, the food that he ate, the manner in which he got around town; all of that wasn't really a big deal until he got around people who were eating and wearing different things, and pulling up in cars that he could only imagine at that point. He had lost focus, unable to realize that they had all ended up in the same place because he was just as smart, if not smarter, than them. Subsequently, it ceased to be about where he would end up, and where he started became more important. Believing that caused people in his neighborhood to stand out for what they had at the moment and how they got it, which in turn attracted his focus and seduced him into abandoning all that truly mattered, what his mother had set him up to be able to achieve from the start. The rest is history, his-story for you.

The third brother allowed the pressure of his peers to shift his focus from learning to read in class in an effort to better himself, to his feelings of inferiority for not being able to do so on their terms. Admitting that, in my opinion, requires a tremendous amount of respect because this is a problem that many people have faced in their lives, and still struggle with to date. As you can see from his letter, the skill of being able to focus was not one that he lacked, it was just applied to the wrong agenda. Once he set his mind to becoming the most important man in his community, nobody could stop him. Had he applied that same focus and determination in the classroom, or stuck it out, he told you himself that he could have been just as successful as he was in building his reputation on the streets, minus all of the heartache and pain that he has had to endure on behalf of those that he lost on his journey, as well as his own family.

Don't make the mistake of losing focus on your dreams. If you drop out of school, you will still have to acquire the same knowledge that you thought you could do without, just in a much more dangerous setting. This means that you will have willingly placed yourself in the front row of the class of a confused teacher, one who likes to give the test before teaching the lesson. This may sound fun, but learning on the fly when you don't have to is dangerous and nerve-wrecking, trust me. Dealing drugs may seem as easy as handing something to another person, but it's much more than that. You may have thought that you were ducking that nagging teacher in math class, but you have to know grams and measurements in order to be an effective drug dealer. Where as you may have gotten a bad grade before, you are now subject to be killed for a mistake in this class.

On a much larger scale, if you were lucky enough to make it big selling your drug of choice, once you decide to stop and go legit by starting a business, how are you going to go about establishing and running it effectively with no education? You will end up hiring some of the same people who may have once been your classmates in college to do things such as invest and manage your money (if you can clean it up!), represent you legally, design your building, etc. In the end, they will have ended up making just as much as you, only without a lot of the head and heartaches that you had to endure along the way.

In addition to that, they will actually be able to keep their's!

If the Feds can prove that all that you've acquired was a result of money from illegal activity, guess what, all of it will be seized and your remaining accounts will be frozen when they come for you. These are some of the things that the best have endured during their time in the game. Don't put yourself on that path.

I mentioned that focus takes discipline, well it also takes courage. We can't be naive to the fact that we may have to lose a few passengers that we thought were on the same page along the way. Not everyone is built to resist temptation on the first round, but you must have the courage to sever any relationships that are already in place should they threaten your dream. At this point, anyone who claims to already know you that chooses to introduce things into your life that contradict what you believe in, isn't really your friend anyway.

It is in the face of these tests that you must keep your focus and keep driving. You have come too far to have someone render all of your hard work void because they refused to invest in themselves. Keep your eyes focused straight ahead, foregoing all shortcuts. You may not reach your destination as fast as others may expect, but you know that success, positive success, doesn't happen overnight. View everything counter-productive as a pothole or an unwanted passenger, making the necessary arrangements to avoid them as you forge ahead.

Though it may be required that you sometimes slow down, it is never appropriate to stop! Keep it moving.

Part Two

Those who may have already made a few mistakes, I put this section together with you in mind. It's never too late to get yourself together, regardless of what anyone says. In addition to the first section, these are four things that you should think about in your down time. If you have survived this long, you have what it takes to change it up.

Chapter Six

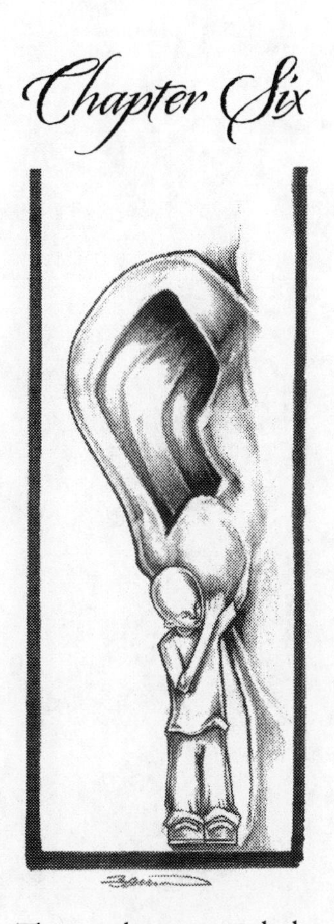

They only want to help.

From: Anonymous

Children Of The World

We pass through this human experience only once. Some errors we live through, others we don't. Parents and elders usually give us the best advice for not making the same mistakes that they did, and so we can reach the heights of our true potential. Therefore, it's important to listen to those who traveled the road that we now travel.

Although there are different levels of the crime life, the results are usually the same—death or prison. In the end, we are robbed of all of our joys. The risks and reward factors will never weigh in our favor, no matter how much we think it one day will.

There is no glory in my story. I was raised by a single parent. My mother was all I had and she did the best that she could with whatever she had. We never had much, so I robbed a bank to get money to buy all the things I thought would make her happy. I bought her her own home, a new car, jewelery, and took her to some of the places that she always wanted to go. I even got married and had my first child. My mom was the proudest grandmother in the world.

I was eventually caught by the police for the second largest bank robbery in the state of North Carolina. I thought I could beat the case so I went to trial. I knew I would win because I had money. Unfortunately, I was wrong. I was convicted and sentenced to twenty-five years.

Within three years, my mother died of a heart condition associated with the depression from my arrest. My only child was placed in foster care, and my child's mother died at the tender age of thirty-three. I lost all of my property, the so-called friends and the people that meant the most to me. Now I'm alone in a cell with regrets of not listening to my elders and making wrong decisions, forcing me to abandon everyone that loved me.

If I could do it all again, I would live a simple life not only with the ones I love, but for the ones that love me.

May 23, 2010

From: Anonymous

To whom it may concern,

I was asked to write a letter in an attempt to talk to young people about life. There's not much I can say about life besides the fact that I've spent half of mine in jail. I've been on death row for 19 years, and I'll be 41 years old soon. I have not seen my family in 20 years, all because I chose the streets over them. As you can see from this letter that I'm writing to you, the streets won.

When I was asked to do this, I said to myself, "What do I tell them?". So I prayed and asked God for some help. The truth is this, some of you have already heard about what will happen to you if you run the streets instead of stay in school. The truth is real, you need to know how beautiful life is. I had counselors in my life that were black and white, genuine good people who wanted the best for me. I can't tell you why I ignored them, maybe because of my attitude. I always looked at it like, "You're not my mother or father!"

What I'm trying to say to you is this: If you have someone in your life who cares for you, listen to them. It doesn't have to be a family member, sometimes words can go a long way. Life is hard, but don't think that you have to shortcut your way through it because you are wrong, there is no such thing. You understand what I'm saying? Don't take this as someone being on death row who's trying to get right with God because that's not the case. When I was your age, someone tried to tell me the same things that I'm trying to tell you, and I ignored them. All they were trying to do was help me.

I hope that you understand my words and take them to the heart because we as people often pay too much attention to the messenger, all the while neglecting the message. I do wish you the best and I will pray for you because I firmly believe that when it's hard, all you have to do is pray and God will help you. Peace and love.

P.S—Today is a good day to be alive because when you can help someone, you should not do it because it's the right thing to do, but because it's what's in your heart. Thank you for letting me share some kind words.

March 24, 2010

Listening

I chose to start the second phase of this book with this topic because I feel that it is a skill that is essential in order for those who have made a few mistakes to be able to make a positive transition. As highlighted in previous chapters, mastering this skill will not be easy, but at the same time, it is not as hard as you may think.

Being young, and constantly moving and shaking in the streets, there are several opportunities for you to listen that usually get either overlooked, or just plain disregarded. From past experience, three major components come to mind, all of which I will share with you.

Outsiders.

Once you have made the successful leap into the underworld that is known as the streets, you will start to notice different things. First, and arguably most important, it will be fairly obvious that the art of communication has been seriously warped somewhere in the middle of where you just came from, and where you now find yourself. From my experience, this warped concept is the product of young people feeling as though they have nothing in common with anyone except those that they hang with. Subsequently, everyone that attempts to approach you with an opinion, no matter how valid, who doesn't share your views about life or a particular situation, is deemed an outsider and is immediately stripped of his/her voice.

At the opposite end of the spectrum, you have those who you know truly love you trying to steer you in the right direction. These people are also treated as outsiders, but for a different reason. They are simply viewed as "playing their part" because we feel that they are obligated to nag at us about things that they know nothing about.

I am here to tell you that both of these views will come back full circle and smack you in the face if you don't adopt a different perspective.

At the very least, when someone approaches you in the streets to pull you up on something that they feel is detrimental to either their personal or community development, or both, you should at least acknowledge the fact that it takes guts. With all of the senseless killings and random acts of violence towards innocent people, it is a wonder that anyone (let alone an outsider) would be encouraged to step to you.

As the saying goes: Everyone has a story to tell. So before you be so quick as to dismiss someone who puts themself at risk in order to tell you a good word or two, stop and take the time to hear their's. You may be very surprised to hear what they have to say about where they have been in life, and it might be in line with where you are heading. People rarely wish bad on other people, despite where they've been and what they've experienced.

The stories in this book should at least be a testament to that. Whether it's a counselor at school, someone else's parent, or the lady that seems to give you a hard time whenever your paths cross, the one thing that they all have in common is that they want to see you do something else, something productive instead of destructive. Though the manners in which they express themselves may vary, the underlying message is still the same. Maybe you could initiate a profound conversation, as well as build a solid relationship with just one simple question: "Why do you care?". I mean come on, you already dwell in a cesspool of multiple personalities, most of which are violent, so you should be able to handle a conversation with an outsider right? I'm sure that them doing you physical harm is the last thing on your mind, so what are you afraid of?

Yourself.

When you first made the decision to enter the streets, you had to get used to the idea of disengaging certain parts of yourself, most of which are emotional. In turn, this opened your mind to be able to accept certain ideologies by way of conversations with your new peers. These new ideologies would mentally prepare you for what was surely waiting behind every corner, so to speak. Surely the central theme of that indoctrination was rooted in truth because the environment that you were willingly about to place yourself in posed dangers that were, and still are, undoubtedly real.

Well, the truth that those who you have deemed as outsiders, and the truth that you know deep down inside, is no different. It's just the overall truth, the truth of what you are really doing to yourself, and what is waiting behind the corner that you will come to once you pass the one that your homeboy warned you about.

You see we like to duck what I call sensible people, the most important being the sensible person that lives inside of us that we constantly suppress for "survival". We do this because they threaten to expose what is real, that which will eventually overshadow what we have come to create in our minds. The simple fact that we do this is evidence that we are very much aware of what we are setting in motion for ourselves.

I'll give you an example of a sensible person and how I destroyed the sensible person inside of me from my personal life.

I often pace back and forth in my cell thinking back to a conversation that I had long ago with a friend of mine that I virtually grew up with. This friend is not, and has never been, involved in the lifestyle that I participated in.

He'd heard that I'd been arrested and was facing the death penalty for a crime that was widely known that I didn't commit in my neighborhood. One morning he came to visit me and told me what the streets were saying, how everyone was talking about who really had committed the crime (which was a murder), but nobody was lifting a finger to do anything for me in terms of helping me secure an efficient lawyer, or send me money so that I could get through the time that I was doing as a result of being incarcerated while fighting the case.

After making all of this known to me, he must have saw the disappointment on my face. I mean these were people that would break their necks to wave at me when I rode by, people that I'd helped on numerous occasions in one way or another. This prompted him to ask me a question that would spark an intense conversation. He asked me why I wouldn't tell the police who really committed the crime in an effort to save my life, a life that apparently nobody else valued? My reply was short, but typical considering the ideologies that had been instilled in me, I couldn't tell.

The look that he gave me, gave me the impression that I had just grew a second head.

"You mean to tell me, that you are willing to sit here and let the government kill you for something that you didn't even do, and the person who really did isn't lifting a finger to help you?" He said.

"I have to, this is the life that I chose." I replied.

"Ain't no way!" He told me, shaking his head in disbelief.

Now as I said before, my friend was not involved in the lifestyle that I was, he was a straight shooter. He is still my friend to this day, and he is a model for sensible people.

Though I stuck to my guns, and received a death sentence for it, I never forgot that conversation for some reason. During my times of introspection, I always tried to look at things from the perspective that he offered me, the perspective of the people that look at you everyday. To them, we are nothing short of fools on a suicide mission. Though I stand by my decision, lets look at things through their eyes for a moment.

I agreed to *die*, to give up my life for a person that made it crystal clear that he wouldn't do the same for me, by going to prison for a crime that I didn't commit. I also made it clear, evidently, that I didn't care about my own life by choosing to indulge in a lifestyle that would require me to do so, just like you.

You would take a cell next door to me right? I mean, once you get locked up, regardless of if it was for something that you did or not, you have to honor your commitment to destroying your life. A man, or woman, is nothing without their word!

But if you know that this not what you want for yourself in the end, if you know that the things that you are doing now have no future, do something! If you decide to change your thinking and/or your habits *before* you get in a position like this, nobody can say anything.

The actions of your peers.

Sometimes actions can scream far louder than words can. Take a moment to analyze your current situation. If you are reading this book while incarcerated somewhere, whether juvenile or adult, ask yourself a few things. Who are the people that are there for you right now, making sure that you have what you need to make it while in your situation? Look around you at the demeanors of some of the inmates who know that they will never see home again, do you want to be like that? Think about some of the people that you would be with right now if you were not incarcerated, where do you see their lives ending up? Analyze their actions, are they more angry than happy, or sad all the time?

These are some of the things that people are reluctant to say, but will show you constantly if you just pay attention.

When you were indoctrinated in the beginning, they didn't tell you everything. They told you that jail was a possibility, but they never informed you that you could be the slickest thing moving out there, evading every trap that is set to catch you, only to end up in a cage for something that you didn't do, stuck because you are a victim of your own reputation. In fact most dudes that are incarcerated are there for something that someone else did, someone who got caught up doing something else and just had to have some company.

To tell you such a thing would most likely reduce your interest initially, if you are a sensible person, thus increasing the odds of what happened to you being much more likely to happen to them. Who in their right mind wants to be stuck in a cell for the rest of their life, while the people that you thought were cool are out running around doing all of the things that you like to do, things that you could still be doing had you decided to do the right thing instead of try to be cool right along with them? When you define what is cool, that makes you a leader. When you let what's cool define you, that makes you stupid!

These are things that outsiders see when they look at you, fools trying to duck reality. These are some of the things that they will bring to your attention, if you will listen for a moment. Don't judge their message by what they look like, or their age, or their relation to you. The fact of the matter is that they will not have to physically die or spend the rest of their life in jail for what you do, you will.

Go inside of yourself and define what is cool, tap into your inner-voice and listen to it. If it feels wrong, it is wrong!

If you are incarcerated and have a chance to get out and try again, develop a better plan. Look at all of your experiences for just what they are through a different lens, and then evaluate them. When that door closes for some people, it will never open again, so show your appreciation by never knocking on it again.

Chapter Seven

They do not define you, how you respond to them does.

From: Anonymous

Pathology—The study of the nature of disease and its causes, processes, development, and consequences.

"Circumstances don't define people, it is the will of a person within life's storms that defines them."

Young Brothers,

My intentions with the words that I scribe are to prevent young brothers from tornadoing along a path of self-destructive behavior. It's important to me to ultimately act as a mirror, reflecting the light of knowledge on young men, so that they can come to realize the pathology that plagues the community.

I currently sit on death row. Like many young boys from urban neighborhoods all over, I was indoctrinated with the street ideology, as well as an inferiority complex. After years of self reflection, I've come to realize that our moral fiber is being molded by hands absent of morality themselves. Warped principles are being instilled in our young brothers, stunting their mental and emotional growth, propelling them into the street life blindly without thorough knowledge of their final destination. They are never given a chance to weigh the consequences that are awaiting them at the end of the crooked journey (jail or the graveyard), only to end up feeling empty and cheated by the people who were supposed to give them their moral compass once they arrive at doom's gates.

Yes, I understand how you can feel that your self worth is rooted in the pursuit of material possessions. I felt like that, and received the same notion that worldly success should be accomplished at any cost, to hell with the effects that it may have on those in close proximity.

That's why it's not uncommon to witness a young brother selling drugs to his own mother, all in the name of the "paper chase".

When the community that is supposed to be nurturing you fails to comprehend the effects of these pathologies that they are imparting onto you, when these diseased ideals are allowed to persist, they leave traces of residue in other parts of your life. Some examples are how we interact with women, the fact that most young brothers in the lifestyle view them as objects or possessions. I've been guilty of this. These corrupt concepts start to fashion certain attributes like selfishness, dishonesty, and greed. They manifest themselves into the overwhelming forces that drive a young person's life. (This is not an excuse, I just want to explain this pathology.)

"I refuse to accept or perpetuate false, negative images of myself or my people, no matter how lucrative the rewards."

Violence Breeds More Violence

The fact remains that it doesn't make sense how black men are murdering each other at astonishing rates. There are piles of data that show that over eight thousand black men are murdered each year. The fact that eighty percent of these homicides are sadly at the merciless hands of other African Americans that have shared the same struggles and historical ancestry is in and of itself terrifying.

Before any of us can sincerely commit to transcending the culture of violence, we must first learn and truly try to understand the root cause of this life ending pathology. I'm sure that we've all observed our peers, the young brother that seems to be frustrated all the damn time, displaying all types of animosity (look at him wrong and he'll take your head off!). Ask yourself a question. How can an individual be transported to a place where they can become emotionally detached from humanity, where violence is their only means of communication, the solution to all of life's problems?

Well, what I'm about to say may shock some (sorry). This pathology was created by an innocent intent, tradition. We relay notions to our young children that they must protect themselves from all insults, verbal and physical, using any means necessary. No kid is born destined to be violent, in my opinion.

Our young boys are feeling like they have been abandoned by the people who gave them life and were supposed to love them unconditionally. Young brother, take a moment to think about your peers that may have a father who is in prison, or who just refuses to be in their life. Then there are those whose mothers are dealing with a drug addiction that is consuming their entire existence. The children are left to fend for themselves. This brings so much pain and despair that a young person may feel like absolutely no one wants them or loves them, and starts to lash out. There is a saying that I'm reminded of at this moment: "What you don't feed will certainly die."

All things living need to be loved, most certainly humans. People thrive when there is a lot of loving people around us. The youth are dying from a lack of emotional and spiritual love. Nobody wants to die, no matter what. Whether physical, spiritual, or emotional, it is universal law: self preservation. People will fight back in the most violent ways, whether killing themselves, or murdering someone else!

"There are so many opportunities open to me, I must first learn to love myself despite my past."

Education is the instrument that can be used to kill all social ills.

I read a study that stated that a large percent of the people that are incarcerated did not graduate from high school. If this happens to be a fact, we as a race should be worried because the dropout rate in our community is twice as high than in any other.

In African American households all over the United States, education is no longer a priority. We seem to have given up on demanding young brothers to read and encouraging them to believe that higher learning is the ticket to achieving any and everything desired in life. Instead we have allowed ignorance of all types to overwhelm our black children.

You do realize that whenever any race of people have more of their men going to prison than college, they are in the midst of a dire situation? An individual that is uneducated has a much higher chance of falling into criminal behavior, being unemployed, and suffering from depression. I'm sure that you've heard the same stories that I have, young brother, about how bad the urban public schools are, teachers not qualified to educate our children, too many kids in the classroom, outdated books, etc. I agree that standards should be improved in our schools for you.

As soon as I made that last statement, I was reminded of a time when black people understood the value that education held. It was and still is, our way to rise above the cesspool of madness and solve the ills of the world. At one time young brother, slaves were denied the access to education. They would literally risk their lives for the possibilities that it created for their future.

Thanks for allowing me the opportunity to come to the table with my thoughts. My goal is just to get you young brothers to identify the pathologies in the above paragraphs. This way you can begin to stop the cycle of this self-destructive behavior.

I was you . . . please don't be me! It will ultimately be in your hands to start and build the emotional and spiritual blocks within yourself to enable you to transcend the paths that our fathers, mothers, and other relatives have taken. I was plagued by the same pathology that you are struggling with, and now I sit on death row. Though these diseases in our communities are complex and have many layers, you can at least see them now and make the proper changes in your life.

Make the changes and live a healthy life, mentally, spiritually, emotionally, and physically, because you can't change if you're not around.

December 22, 2010

From: Anonymous

G, what's up big homie? Here's my message to the youth that you asked me to write. I apologize for taking so long to write it, I just been so busy writing my book and this album that I'm putting together. I'm proud of you though for taking the initiative to start this much needed movement . . .

"My Hood To Your Hood"

Growing up in this struggle, we can't help being the way we are. I guess we're just a product of our environment. In my hood, it ain't nothing nice. You got guys throwing up sets, slinging stones, and clapping guns. And I'm not even talking about the grown folks. In my hood guys get murdered and die on a regular basis, sometimes over something as petty as who gets to hustle on what corner. I guess it's like a territorial thing, you know, how dogs and other animals mark their territory by pissing on it. Same principle. We piss in the very spots where we lay our heads. But does that make us animals? You be the judge.

The way it's set up, we're left to police and govern ourselves, but as soon as we do something that affects the world outside of our hoods, the law be all in our asses. Where was they when my little cousin just caught it in the back last month? Where was they when my best friend took them shells going to the store to get a dutch? Where was they when them clowns tried to blow my head off for a chain? A lot of times, we do the things we do because that's what's programmed in us, passed down from parent to child to child and so on. This kind of shit goes on day in and day out in my hood.

What I just ran down to you sounds familiar, don't it big homie? It should because I'll bet if you ask your cousins, they'll say the same shit is going on. From my hood to your hood big homie, it's the same old thing. So why don't we act like it and try to do something about it? G, my little cousin just got his head blown off big homie, I received a letter from my aunt last week telling me about what happened! G, my whole family turned their backs on me because of him. My other aunt, his mother, hates my guts for putting my hands on him when I was trying to be a big brother to him when I saw them on the corner trying to hustle. I was only trying to look out for the family! Now look what happened, my little homie is dead!

They need us out there G. Our people are lost big homie. We can better lead them because now we can think more. We've been around and learned things that only come from great minds. I'm blessed because God has allowed me to meet strong men like you who opened up my eyes. I love you comrade. Keep your head up and always remember that hard times don't last, real men do. I hope this helps homie.

From: Anonymous

A Message To Our Youth

Growing up in the poor inner-city ghetto, violence and drugs were the most rampant way of life. Drug dealers were the superstars, welfare recipient, single parent young ladies were the groupies, and little children like I was were the fans. Despite having dreams of escaping the ghetto, I followed in the footsteps of the superstars I had once admired. Unfortunately, but unsurprisingly, I am on death row now, and have been for over 18 years.

Eighteen years of lockdown, which is the typical living condition of death row confinement, has brought me into confrontation with myself. I began to discover that my life, like an onion, had many layers surrounding it's core. Those layers were projected images that bellied my true identity. Recognizing the nature of those layers began the process of dismantling those lies, but victory wasn't consummated until I discarded them. My purpose for writing is to impart a fraction of the wisdom that I have learned from this process in hopes of preventing the next generations from repeating the mistakes of the past.

As a young teenager, my passion for education was brutally assaulted by the ridicule of my peers, mainly because of the raggedy clothes and shoes that I wore to school. This lead me to replace my passion for school, which I knew was my ticket out of poverty, with a passion for fast money. "Fast money", I reasoned, "will enable me to escape the ridicule of my peers and, most importantly, be considered one of the superstars of the inner-city." As a result, I dropped out of school and pursued the street life. This tragic mistake, trading my education for the street life, began the formation of the "layers" that inevitably lead me to death row.

As time progressed I started to think that illegal money, as well as drugs and women, was the life, but this was a lie and was quickly shattered when the possessions I had accumulated did not bring me the fulfillment I had expected. To my surprise, the opposite had come about: discontentment.

To my surprise, the path I had taken to the top was quite destructive. It was one of self-hatred! The more I hated myself, the more area I conquered, and the more people I destroyed along the way. Even the people that I befriended didn't really love me; they only wanted me for what they could get. This only added more fuel to my self-hatred and, as a result, my hatred for others. I have now learned that it is impossible to love others without first loving yourself.

I have finally rekindled my love for education and, therefore, discovered that love is the only foundation that a truly fulfilled life can be built upon. If I had learned this before the countless bad decisions I had made, I would have never sold drugs. True love will never hurt others; hence, love must be the only force that empowers our actions and reactions, not our self-destructive egos.

As I began to grow in love for myself, I learned that knowledge by itself is reckless; it must be guided and developed in wisdom. Wisdom is basically applying knowledge rightly. Even so, knowledge guided in wisdom, as well as a religious foundation, will empower you to ascend the heights of heaven. There is no goal or aspiration which cannot be accomplished. I am living proof of this truth, for I am, in part fulfilling my dreams through this letter: Educating the youth so that they will become a force on the earth, a force that doesn't repeat the mistakes of the previous generation, but heeds this admonition: "Those who fail to learn from history are doomed to repeat it."

August 12, 2010

It's Only The Beginning

I was prepared to begin this chapter with all kinds of statistics that I have read about you being less likely to be able to make it if you are from a certain area, or your race being of the ultimate importance, but I have changed my mind.

Believe it or not, you are in total control of what happens to you, or what doesn't happen for that matter. It doesn't matter if you can look outside of your window and see green grass or brown dirt, a picket fence or a steel gate, your future is what you want it to be.

So many people develop the idea that things like these determine who you are as a person, but that couldn't be further from the truth. Some would love for you to believe that because you come from impoverished beginnings, or a rough neighborhood, or a "broken family", that you are somehow inferior to those who have been fortunate enough to experience the opposite.

While I do believe that humble beginnings like those will give you a unique perspective on life and how to go about it, I also happen to believe that this is not necessarily a bad thing.

You see, starting from where society likes to refer to as the bottom gives you an early lesson in something that many people lack today, humility. This champions you for something that everyone is certain to experience in life, adversity. Everybody wants to win, but nobody likes to acknowledge the fact that in order for someone to win, someone has to lose. Grant it, you don't have to stay a loser, but losing is a part of life. You will hear the word no, doors will not always open on the first try, you will not always have the money to do whatever you want, etc. There are no exceptions to this rule, I don't care if you are Oprah Winfrey, Donald Trump, Carlos Slim, or whoever else you can think of.

Now of course being a winner is wonderful, if you look at it unilaterally. But if you stop and think about it, if you start out winning, running through everything that gets in your way, humility can move farther and farther away from your grasp. Until you have suffered a loss, or faced adversity, can you actually say that you have been tested to see if you can actually handle a loss in life? No. Losing builds character, which is an amalgamation of a few important things like empathy, humility, resilience, drive, and so on. These are the things that make up a true winner because winners are meant to inspire people, not tear them down. To inspire someone is to motivate them to go inside themselves and see a winner, not to step on the fingers of those who are trying hard to pull themselves up.

Starting out from a less than desirable position should not cause you to beat yourself up or feel inferior to those who are a little more well off. Your humble beginnings are actually a blessing in disguise because you have started out with some of the pressures that life is certain to impose on you, and you are taking it. In other words, you are experienced in that area, and once you successfully make it out of the conditions that you find yourself despising, you will appreciate where you end up much more than those around you because you have seen the other side. You know that you can handle the ridicule that comes with not having the best clothes, or the shame that comes with not having enough food or money, etc. This makes *you* a winner because you have a story to tell that has depth. You also know that those who are causing the grief have never really been tested because if they had, they would know that it takes strength that is unrivaled by anything in this world to be able to get up and do whatever has to be done everyday in the face of these temporary conditions.

Your experiences, coupled with the knowledge of their ignorance should give you the drive to want to change your situation for the better, the right way. More people have done it than not, without putting themselves in a detrimental position, it's just that you don't pay attention when they tell you. Your failure to hear what is being said due largely in part to the fact that you are too busy **semi**-analyzing what you *see* (remember that?).

The majority of your favorite stars come from very humble beginnings. They've experienced it all, from barely having food on the table, sharing clothes with siblings, having one or both parents incarcerated or killed, to hearing gun shots and seeing people killed on a daily basis in their impoverished neighborhoods, but they championed through it. They used those experiences as motivation to go out and fulfill what they knew was their purpose in this world, determined to change the lives of those who shared their plight, whether family or friends, as well as themselves.

But you don't notice that, you just think that they magically appeared on your television screens huh? You don't listen when they try to tell you indirectly, all you see is the end result, the glory days.

Those of you who decide to skip school and ride around listening to Lil' Wayne, missed the part where he confessed to being a great student, or that his mother wouldn't have let him rap if his grades weren't in order. He openly expressed in an interview that he couldn't understand how kids whine that school is so hard when you have a teacher telling you to find answers that are already written down for you in a book. But you missed that, you're just too busy riding around bobbing your heads while he indirectly calls you all idiots for not taking advantage of an important opportunity.

Now we also can't be naive to the fact that, like you, there are artists who have made a few mistakes on their rise to the top. While they have been fortunate, they too constantly share their experiences with you, some through their work and others in conversation.

One such artist is Jeezy. He openly expresses the fact that he almost didn't make it to stardom, having narrowly escaped a huge drug conspiracy. I guess you were more concerned with the beat while he constantly expressed the pain of losing those that he loves due to the lifestyles that they chose, and how he would trade it all to get their freedom back.

Two more examples are Biggie and T.I, and I believe that they are the most profound because they involve the rational thinking of other people. You would have never had the blessing to hear either of these talented individuals had they not made the decision to part with the day to day activities that consumed so much of their early years in an attempt to get to work with the people that would prove to be pivotal in their careers.

For Biggie, that person was Diddy. He begged him not to be confined to his neighborhoods perception of "the way out" when he decided to go out of town and sell drugs in another state. Promising to make him a star, which was his dream, he convinced him to come back and weather the storm with perseverance so that he could eventually become a successful rapper and businessman, and he did.

For T.I. it was Jason Geter and DJ Toomp, two people who refused to invest their time and energy into someone who was bound for prison or the graveyard, thus giving him an ultimatum. He ended up making the right choice, and the rest is history. Even now he is still reminded of the life that he left behind because whenever he makes a bad decision, he goes to jail.

The common thread here is that all these people had it rough coming up, and some even chose the wrong route initially, but they realized that they had no real chance at success with the way that they were heading. Grant it some of them had a little outside help, but hopefully this reminder will do something for you. I am sure that you will be able to channel all that you have endured, and use it to propel you toward your dream. Once you do this, you too will encounter people that will be willing to help you get to where you want to be, but I can assure you that no successful person is going to lift a finger until it looks like you want to help yourself in a way that is destined for longevity.

Turning to the streets is not the answer to your dilemma, trust me. Being a street dude is more implanted than taught, most of us pick it up from our surroundings, family, and friends. Just because you are born under a deep-rooted family tree, doesn't mean that you are content with living under it. You can be the difference-maker.

Where you are right now is only temporary if you choose to focus on where you're going. Those that take pride in kicking you while you're "under" them, or so they think, will eventually end up "under" you if you want them to be. Nobody starts out on top, if they did then it was because someone before them walked through the mud in order to be able to put them on the pedestal that they may or may not be taking for granted. If you are going to use your circumstances as an excuse to inflict pain on someone else by selling them drugs, robbing them, or flat-out killing them, then call it exactly what it is, an excuse.

As you can see from the letters in this chapter, many of the brothers believed the same thing that you have come to accept, directly or indirectly. They looked to the exterior for everything, their neighborhoods, their clothes, their peers, etc., and thought that what they saw was what was inevitably meant for them. The first brother defined that as a pathology, your perception of your current predicament and it's causes, as well as it's development.

The second brother believed that if he wasn't fly by other people's standards then he wasn't nothing. He now knows how wrong his perception was, a lesson that he had to learn in a place where everyone has to wear the same thing.

The third brother gave you a direct look into his life on the streets and the thought patterns that govern them. As you can see, he ended up in prison, where he was forced to take the time to understand the pathology that had inadvertantly influenced his own life.

All of these men are examples of what can happen if you let your circumstances define you, instead of the other way around. They are also champions because they have walked through the fire in order to gain the experience that they've shared with you, in an effort to place you on a pedestal that you hopefully won't take for granted.

Make the best of it!

Chapter Eight

You only get so many chances,
then the hammer comes down!

From: Anonymous

There are many different ways that a person can come to crime. For some, its roots lie in poverty. Growing up poor, hungry, and having nothing can build in a person the burning desire to succeed, to be free of a certain neighborhood, or way of life, at any cost, to never do without again. But for most in that position, there will never be opportunities such as attending college, starting a business, or going to work for a big corporation. The only real option they can see to find success is through slinging drugs, or picking up a gun to take what they need.

Others come to crime through laziness, or greed. While they may or may not have had the opportunities to get ahead in other ways, they choose a life of crime usually because of an unwillingness to work for what they desire, or from believing that they can't earn by work as much as they can by breaking law.

But as for most of my own personal friends, they found their way to prison by a different route. Though any one of them may have also been poor, lazy, or greedy, the actual road here was paved with small things. Things that they really didn't regard as crimes at all until it was too late.

Have you ever been out with your friends, feeling good, feeling kind of rowdy, and had one of them say, "Hey, it would be really cool if you did that!"? Of course the "that" to which they are referring to is always going to be something illegal; stealing something, breaking something, or whatever. At the time, it probably did feel like something to do, a crazy stunt which would give everyone a laugh. It certainly didn't seem like any sort of crime, now did it? But the thing is, most cops don't have much of a sense of humor, and neither does the law. No matter how funny what your friends wanted you to do seemed at the time, the cops and the courts won't take that into account, and you will still get hammered for it.

The same goes for the things you might do to earn respect. While you may not necessarily be thinking of what you did to impress your friends or your girl in terms of how it broke the law, you can bet that someone else is looking at it that way. And once you find yourself on the cops radar, once you have any conviction at all on your record, no matter how petty it seems, your life is headed downhill from there.

You may be scoffing at my words right now, and thinking of people you know, or have heard of, who have become successful after having been in prison. They do exist, and I probably know a good many of the people you are thinking of too. But they are the exception, not the rule. The vast majority of people with prison records never find any sort of success in life, economical or otherwise. Not because they don't have the ability, but because so many doors are closed to them that they have no choice but to fail.

Many people are aware that once you have a felony conviction, you can no longer vote or legally own a gun. But most don't know that there are a lot of other restrictions as well. Did you know that in some states, if you're a felon, you can't even work in the food industry? That some states don't allow felons to work in construction? At least one state that I know of doesn't allow felons to have a driver's license. Most of the major trade guilds for carpenters, electricians, plumbers, truck drivers, and more, don't allow felons to join. There are banks that won't give felons a loan, businesses that won't give them credit, or cash their checks, landlords who won't rent to them, the list is just about endless.

So once you take these first few steps, it often turns out that even if you wanted to, you can never go back. Crime becomes the only option that you have, since you can't make it with a real job. And if you think that you will always be able to make money that way, guess again. Once the system has it's hooks in you, it doesn't like to let go. If you think you can get away because you're young, thinking that you will only get a slap on the wrist, those days are over. As of July 2009, there were 6,807 juveniles serving life sentences in prison. Juries have no problem at all slamming you forever, regardless of your age.

Let's look at crime from two different angles for a moment.

First, think of things logically. For those who believe that they are bound to make more money from crime than they ever could by working a straight job, look at some facts: (NOTE: Some of these numbers may have changed, but the underlying point is still the same.) A minimum wage job at a fast food restaurant, which you hate to imagine yourself doing, would bring in about $15,000 a year. The average bank robbery brings in about $2,800, and only takes a few minutes. The robbery seems like the smart choice right? Wrong! Keep looking at the statistics. Ninety-four percent of all bank robbers are caught within twenty-four hours, and the average sentence they receive is nine years. That means that if you hid or spent the money before the cops got you, and they didn't get any of it back, the amount from the robbery ($2,800) is all that you will earn in the next nine years. Do the math, that's almost $300 a year. Is it worth the nine years that you will lose? Had you worked a minimum wage job ($15,000 a year), you would have earned $135,000 in that same time frame, and kept your freedom as well. Which one of these choices is looking like the best now?

I wish that I could offer the same statistics for drug dealing, but it varies too much. I can tell you this though, for every fifty dudes selling drugs, only one is pulling down any real amount of money. Of those major players, only maybe one out of a hundred make it out of the game, and get to enjoy what they made. The rest are in prison, with me. I have met a lot of guys over the years who made major amounts of money on the streets selling drugs, most are now dead broke. They spent the money just as fast as it came in, never forseeing a day when they would not be making more. Either that or the cops got it all, or maybe the lawyers, or they got burned for it by the very people that they trusted after coming to prison. Whatever the reason, the money is gone now. As for those who did manage to hang on to some, well, they can only spend the same amount in the prison store that everyone else is limited to each week. So in the end, the money really didn't mean a thing.

Now I will mention some of my own experiences, for any who may doubt what I said earlier about how the system doesn't like to let go once it has you. I was arrested when I was 19, for a crime that occurred when I was 18. As it was my first conviction, I only received sixteen months. Not that I was thrilled about losing over a year of my life, but I still figured it wasn't much. I would do the time and come out a whole new man, tougher, stronger, and with more respect. Only it didn't work out that way. Before I could get out, I was hit with another charge. Then another. Then another. Now, I'm 39 years old. I have been locked up longer than I had been alive when I was first arrested. I never did make it back to the streets, not even once, since I picked up that original conviction. Sixteen months turned into 3 life sentences, and 2 death sentences. The only thing that is going to set me free is the needle that is going to be shoved in my arm while I'm strapped to a gurney, sometime in the next few years.

No one can say that I don't know what I'm talking about when I tell you that the system doesn't like to let you go.

The next time someone tells you that it would be cool for you to swipe a car and go joyriding, or shoplift something for a laugh, stop and think about it. If it would make you so cool, why don't they do it, instead of suggesting it to you? There is nothing "cool" or "funny" about being locked up in a cell the size of a bathroom, with everything that you can have or do being dictated to you by someone else.

Anyway that you look at it, the road that I've walked is no way to go. Take it from someone who knows, who has seen their wasted life slide by. Whatever options are open to you, there is always something better than the one which will end with you in prison.

It's Not Worth It!
April 12, 2010

From: Anonymous

The Future,

I was born and raised in Baltimore City. I grew up in a rough and depressed environment. Me and my brother were raised in a single parent household. I hardly saw my mother because she was usually working two or three jobs and sometimes attending college to try to improve our conditions. So my brother and I were usually there to raise ourselves. I participated in some of the gross acts that was considered to be cool in the neighborhood like stealing, robbing, and carrying a gun, not to mention fighting. As I got older and saw the other kids making money through selling drugs, I tried my hand at what I considered to be a road to the American dream.

At the age of twenty-two, I was arrested and spent the next eight years in prison. I came home at age thirty and through bad association, was arrested again. I thought because I was living a crime free life that that would insulate me from problems but through the wrong association (so-called friends) I was arrested again. As I became a man, I realized how much I have destroyed my life and how much time I've wasted doing negative things. As a result of my incarceration, I missed the opportunity to raise my kids like a responsible father and become an asset to my family by being there for them. I've missed out on a lot of normalities in life. I've experienced family members passing, close friends being tragically murdered, as well as losing close friends and family to life sentences in prison. Many of them felt like they were following in my footsteps, not realizing that those were steps of destruction.

Now I'm trying to repair all of the mistakes that I've made in life. I now realize the importance of education and staying focused on positivity. With a criminal record, there are many things that I will never be able to do like work certain jobs, or bear arms. In some states you can't even vote with a criminal record. So my opportunities are somewhat limited. I have to try twice as hard compared to the average man.

I look at successful people who in their tender twenties became multi-millionaires like Steve Jobs (Apple), Bill Gates and Paul Allen (Microsoft), Sergey Brin and Larry Page (Google), Jawed Karim, Chad Hurley and Steven Chen (You Tube), and Mark Zuckerburg (Facebook). I mention these people because the only thing that separates them from me is that I didn't apply myself in a positive manner. Today these people are still thriving in the world, while guys like myself who chose to live a life of crime are compounded with problems like prison, tragic murders, kidnappings for ransom, and being robbed, not to mention our families who are sometimes drug into these same dilemmas. Success is not always defined by your net worth, but sometimes by your intelligence and/or your heart. Any brainless person can break law, but it takes an intelligent person to live a successful life through education, hard work, and perseverance.

I see now that a lot of the company that I kept and the places that I frequented were significant contributors to my shortcomings. When I decided to change my people, places, and things, I was finally able to live a happy stress-free life. About one percent of criminals make it successfully, but I'm sure that they still have endured plenty of other issues along the way. I've spent over twelve years of my adult life in prison and would dare anyone that thinks he can handle this to try, we can certainly trade places. If you want to enjoy life and be successful, then don't follow what I've done, but rather listen to my advice.

April 20, 2010

From: Anonymous

I promised my mother that I would always be there for her. I was raised in an environment where abuse ran rampant. There were many days and nights where as a child, I sat huddled in a corner, hugging my older brother, shaking and fearful that my stepfather would turn his wrath on us as soon as he got through beating my mother to a bloody pulp, only a few feet away.

And yes, my fear was justified. That evil bastard would beat me black and blue . . . with belts, belt buckles, sticks, his fists . . .

I was ten years old when my mother shot him six times. That's when the abuse stopped, but by then it was too late, I was severely damaged. I had suffered immensely from the trauma. It was so hard for me to trust people, my one true security was the knowledge that now I knew how to fight back, I knew how to protect myself, and my mother.

"Mama, I will always be here for you." I said, and I meant it. I would always be there for her, or so I thought . . .

My mother worked two to three jobs to support her five kids. As a result, she was never home. I didn't have anyone to motivate me to do what was right, my mentors became the old cats in my hood who lived and died by that thug life. My school was the school of hard knocks where science, english, etc. was substituted for the dope game. I learned my math by counting greenbacks in a project breezeway.

But that was just a small side of that thug life. The most significant and damning was the loss of life. By the time I was fourteen, all of my friends were dead. The streets were claiming lives swiftly and without mercy. It seemed like everyday another one was biting the dust. Chills would traverse my spine as mothers would stand in crowds screaming: "Oh God, not my baby!", and I would look around until I saw my own mother. She would be standing there watching me intently, undoubtedly thinking: "Thank you Lord, thank you for not taking my baby." I wanted to walk over and hug her. I wanted to say: "Mama, I told you that I would always be here." I wanted to, but I didn't.

I wish I would have, those were the times when I needed her the most. I know I promised her that I would always be there, but that was one promise that I failed to keep.

At the age of fourteen I was sent to T.Y.C, the Texas Youth Commission. T.Y.C. was prison for delinquent kids. I escaped three times, before finally completing my bid on October 3, 1989.

I'd told my mother that I would always be there . . . Now I was home.

I was fifteen years old, almost sixteen when I met a young lady that gained my interest. She was eighteen, and beautiful. She had a boyfriend that was her age, but he couldn't accept the fact that he'd lost his girl to this "boy". He shot at me, and shot her in the leg. By that time, my name was ringing like a telephone around the hood. My reputation as a bad boy was solid. The crazy thing about this was that although everyone knew my name, no one really knew who I was. People would be standing right there in my presence saying he's this and he's that . . . so-n-so shot at him, he is going to get that boy.

But I didn't get him. I'd told my mother that I would always be there, and I knew that if I'd retaliated, I couldn't fulfill my promise. However, months later, he pulled a gun on me again. This time, I strapped up and went to get him . . .

I missed him. The bullet struck his father in the head. It was so sad, I couldn't keep my promise to my mother.

Twelve days after my eighteenth birthday, I copped an eight year bid in T.D.C., the Texas Department of Corrections. It took me eight years day for day to make it back home. When that Greyhound bus pulled into the bus station in my hometown on July 30, 2000, I breathed a sigh of relief. At the age of 26, I was home again . . .

I'd told my mother that I would always be there, now I was back. A month later, my past came back to haunt me. A drug dealer paid this guy to kill me.

The first day, I almost fell victim to his .40 caliber, I barely escaped. When he came back the next day, I was forced to shoot back; a bullet to the lung sent him to I.C.U . . . The guy was already wanted for shooting another guy, but as soon as the hospital stapled him up, he escaped. When the police caught up to him he pulled a gun on the cop and took his gun. He was dangerous, and he wanted me more than ever. Unfortunately for me, the police wanted me too. In their eyes, I didn't have the right to defend myself. At the end of October 2000, they kicked in my cousins's door and carted me off to jail for attempted murder.

I made bond, but in November some drug dealers lied and said that I'd robbed them. I ran until January 2001. For almost a year I languished in jail on attempted murder, aggravated robbery, and a host of other charges. When the state realized that their charges against me wouldn't hold, they pushed the Feds to pick up a gun charge for a nine millimeter that they found under a mattress when I was arrested on the attempted murder charge . . .

There was no reasoning with the Feds. They had me and that was all that mattered to them.

Restless and wanting desperately to be free, I escaped again. That same night, one of my girlfriends shot and killed another one of my girlfriends. When they caught me eighteen days later, they charged me with the murder. DNA, forensics, and everything exonerated me, but the Feds didn't care, they just wanted me. They gave the girl that committed the murder, and my former best friend, immunity to lie and say that I told them that I'd committed the murder. Despite the fact that both "witnesses" gave several conflicting alibi's for the time of the murder (both conspired to hide the car that they were in so it couldn't be tested by the forensics lab, and the girl had written a letter four months prior to the murder saying that she would kill the girl), the government proceeded to trial with two liars as their star witnesses. In order to give their case false substance, the government also hired some inmates whom I had never seen before, to lie and say that I'd confessed to them as well. Based on this "evidence", the jury returned a verdict of death.

Now I may never get to keep my promise to my mother . . .

As I sit here on Federal Death Row reflecting upon my life, I've come to realize that I didn't live the life that I did because I wanted to, but simply because that is what I was taught. It was all that I knew.

I wish that someone would have took the initiative and shook me; I wish they would have said: "Sherman wake up, there's more to life than this."

I often think of my mother standing at the crime scenes of my friends, tears in her eyes, thanking the Lord that it wasn't me, her baby, lying there dead in the street. But this time it is her baby, but a thug didn't murder me, the United States Government did.

Mama, I'm sorry that I couldn't keep my promise. Maybe in the next life I will be able to. I promise you, I'll always be there for you . . . Next time.

January 8, 2011

Chances

Take a moment to reflect on your life up to this point.

I'm sure that the amount of times that you've been caught for doing something wrong doesn't even come close to the amount of times that you've got away.

Do you honestly believe that it will always be that way?

The criminal justice system is very sly with the way that it sets it traps for those who believe that they are smarter than the rest. It often disguises the phrase "getting away", obscuring it behind circumstances like you getting probation for an offense, or you getting a little bit of jail time for something that you could have gotten hammered for. Grant it, some people do escape in the wind, never to even pop up on the radar of the law for things that they have done, but it is rare. Most people get jammed up, and end up taking a plea agreement for a lesser sentence, thinking that they too have gotten away due to a lack of evidence, or whatever other reason.

This does nothing but build foolish confidence.

You see it's human nature to feel as though you are "slick" when you do something that you know you're not supposed to and manage to get away with it. This causes you to not think twice whenever you are faced with a situation that grants you the opportunity to revert back to that previous experience. Everyone knows that, from the police, all the way up to the judge that gives you your first few slaps on the wrist. Well, maybe not everyone, more like those who stop and think.

Those who have seen the pattern time and time again, quickly recognize a cocky person when they see one. From that point forward it's just a matter of patience for them, and backward progress for you. In other words, they just keep giving you chances to get it right, chances that they know that you won't recognize because you are not in the right frame of mind to make rational decisions, or analyze situations properly.

As my anonymous brother quickly pointed out to you, the road to prison, or the cemetary, is not paved with quick steps. It is a low and slow process, ensuring that when you finally do end up in a situation where you find yourself in the former, they will be able to keep you there because you have built up quite a resume for yourself.

If you are reading this section of the book and it applies to you, if you have managed to stay out of the sticky hands of the law, it's not too late for you. Even if you are currently in prison and you have a chance to get back out into society, it's not too late. All you have to do is sit back and reflect on your life, recall every situation that you've ever escaped from, only to put yourself right back in it the next day (or for most of us, the same day!). Do you really think that it's going to continue to be that way? Will you always be that lucky? Do you really want to take that type of a gamble, one that will cost you your life, one way or another?

Of course not!

Regardless of whatever world you currently reside in, whether you are in the streets up to your knees, or trapped in the microcosm of that world, prison, you know that it is not a joke. Many people have died in both for petty things. If you have a chance to remove yourself from a path that will continuously lead you to death, why would you constantly take it for granted. Many of you have friends, family members, and even parents that are in prison or the cemetary, first hand examples of what you can expect, yet you believe that you know something different. We often use these people as excuses in an attempt to validate our behavior or our mindstate, but that just makes us look and sound even more stupid. It's one thing when you are doing something without no real example of the consequences that you can expect, in that aspect, you are really just feeling things out (that excuse was free!). But when you have people around you who have constantly experienced the repercussions of an action that you are making, sharing their experiences with you, that is a different story. If you pay attention and take their advice for what it is, or even your own past experiences, then you are gaining wisdom, decreasing your chances of landing in the same situation and getting the same result. Now if you just shrug it off, telling yourself that either they, or you, did something wrong in the process of whatever the action was that landed you in a dilemma, then you are just being hard-headed. That means you are intentionally going out of your way to place yourself on a path that will result in your stagnation, by way of prison or death. That makes you an idiot!

The brothers in this chapter have shared their experiences with the law with you, in an attempt to open your eyes to the many chances, or blessings that you are receiving. They have went out of their way to chronicle some of their own chances, some spanning years in between. Do any of their stories sound familiar? I know that they do because even though they are from three totally different areas in the country, their experiences are very similar. Hopefully this will eliminate whatever excuse you are currently entertaining and re-route you onto a path that will ensure and not arrest your development. The chance that you have right now, might be the last chance that you have to get it right; for yourself, for your family, for your kids, and for those who you have lost on your journey up to this point. The next time could present something totally different to you.

You could get locked up, possibly for something that you didn't even do, and receive a life sentence because of the believeable reputation that you've built for yourself. Think about that, **a life sentence** in a cell much like the one that my anonymous brother described as being the size of a bathroom, having to live with another man. That means that you will never be able to go where you want again, never be able to do what you want again, eat what you want again!

Or something that is much simpler, you could be killed. You could step outside of your house with the intention of coming back and end up getting shot, stabbed, strangled, beaten to death, run over, set on fire (it happens), etc. Or you can get a mixture of the two, you can get locked up for something minor, receive a sentence that you can actually do, and get killed in prison in either a direct beef, a riot, a race war, or a simple misunderstanding (that happens too).

The choice is your's and your's only.

It's not about whether you can handle it or not, or trying to scare you into doing right, it's about recognizing the obvious. It's about realizing how good you have it, while you can still do something about it. If you've managed to make it this far in a game as dirty as the one that you are playing, imagine what you can do in one where the chances of you being murdered or locked up are significantly decreased. The focus that you once dedicated to ducking those perils would be shifted to doing something that you can actually have longevity in, making you unstoppable!

Chapter Nine

Your way obviously isn't working.

From: Anonymous

Salutations Fam,

All praises are due to Allah, who has inspired my young brother G to put this book together for you, and for inspiring me to be able to pass on these gems.

There are 2,243,000 people incarcerated.

If you are reading or listening to these jewels, then you have become a part of this movement, a prevalent movement that I recognize as change and growth. I am sincerely proud of you for joining this journey.

Before I begin, it is important to know that we are a family. One that understands that we are not perfect, that we are prone to mistakes as human beings. These things do not make us bad people. This is what change and growth is all about, understanding yourself. Mistakes are lessons to be learned, and lessons learned play a big part in the change and growth process.

Today I address you as a changed man by the will of God, but I admit that this change did not come easy. In fact, it took me thirty years. You can call me a late bloomer, but I only want it to take you until the end of what you are either reading or listening to at this moment.

This isn't about being scared straight. I'm not here to shake you into reality because you and I live it everyday. We are all statistics, products of either success or failure. It's your choice. Are you a game-changer, or are you #13567039, or worse (DOA)? This is how powerful your mind is, you have a choice.

I speak to you from the depths of the beast, death row, as I sit here awaiting my fate. For me it's simple, kill me today, so that I can live in you tomorrow.

You are my future doctors, lawyers, judges, engineers, teachers, artists, singers, songwriters, professors, and thanks to change and growth, even presidents. Game-changers, the ones who make a difference, this is how we see you.

Now if you don't see yourself as a game-changer, then you can do as we did and cut corners, only to be introduced as number 2,244,000 (Take a look at the number in the beginning). Don't be like me or any of those who tried to cut corners, we all have lost. Truth is, I'm trying to be like you, the one who has a chance to make a difference out there, where it counts.

If only I were you!

February 26, 2011

From: Anonymous

Transformation

I title this transformation because without a true transformation, there can never be a true change in the life of a person who is bound by a life of sin.

Nearly twelve years have passed since I have submitted to the law of transformation in the form of accepting Christ Jesus as my lord and savior. It is through him that I have been able to break free from the bondage of sin. I repented of my sins and have been forgiven by God of all my trespasses, and I am able to live, truly live, the life that scripture says God ordained for me.

My prior form of living was actually only existing from day to day, looking for materialistic things (women, drugs, alcohol, diamonds, cars) to compensate for the emptiness that derived from the deathstyle in which many of us call a lifestyle. I call the life we (I) lived a deathstyle because everything I surrounded myself with could have easily brought about death, if not for the grace of God, because the wages of sin is death, but the gift of God is life eternal. Everyday of my life involved in that deathstyle required me to carry a gun, which could have easily cost me or someone else their life. Drug dealing is made to look glamorous, however, from the moment you begin to indulge in it, you subject yourself to the possibility of losing your life. These are the results of those who choose to involve themselves in the deathstyle way of living, and that is from the least to the greatest. And without a true transformation taking place, this is the end result.

I was once constrained to this way of dying and subjected everyone under my influence—man, women, and child—to that very way of dying. But now, because of the great love in which God has shown me through the love of Jesus Christ, I am compelled to show that very love unto others, which is my life pursuit. God has since delivered me from two life sentences plus thirty years; which left me with fifty-five years, but he didn't stop there. He took two sentences of twenty-five and thirty years and converged them both, producing a single sentence of thirty years overall. However, he didn't stop there, but has now provided an avenue of restoration and deliverance which will allow me, by the grace of God to return home this year of 2010.

If I had to sum this experience up, I would say as the apostle Paul has said: "When I was a child, I thought as a child, spoke as a child, and understood as a child. But when I became a man, I put childish things behind me." (1 Corinthians 13:11); that is, I submitted to the transformation of God and acknowledged as the apostle did when he stated the following: "I press on toward the goal, forgetting what is behind and straining toward what is ahead, toward the prize for which God has called me heavenward in Christ Jesus." (Philippians 3:13-14). Why? Because I have been saved for a purpose, and this is the reason: "Here is a trustworthy saying that deserves full acceptance: Christ Jesus came into the world to save sinners—of whom I am the worst. But for that very reason, I was shown mercy so that in me, the worst of sinners, Christ Jesus might display his unlimited patience as an example for those who believe in him and receive eternal life." (1 Timothy 1:15-17)

I am convinced and compelled to live that righteous life for these reasons and many more, and implore others to do the same because God is no respecter of persons. If he did it for me, he'll do it for you. All you have to do is confess your sins unto him and believe that he sent Jesus Christ, his only begotten son, to die for your sins, and you shall be saved. (John 3:16)

Be Blessed!
May 15, 2010

From: Anonymous

Parish or Everlasting Life: To The Youth

Praise The Lord,

If I could retrace my footsteps, what would I change about my life? Nothing! I say that because I found out that through life's journey, you are going to have trials and tribulations; good days and bad days; as well as ups and downs, but it is not how you start the race, but rather how you finish it (The righteous falls seven times but picks himself back up). We are fighting an enemy that we can't see, and he's been tricking the world for years (The greatest trick Satan ever pulled off was to have or make people think that he doesn't exist).

As God's creation, we need to find out the true meaning/purpose of life. He created us to praise him with all of our heart, mind, body, and soul, and until the day that we truly decide to surrender every thing over to him, we will forever be lost. He said: "I'm the truth, way, and life." We have been following the wrong way of life. The world, our families, friends, environment, communists, government, ourselves, "man": these things will fail but God, he will never fail you. He said that "He so loved the world that he gave his only begotten son and whoever believes in him shall be saved."

May 14, 2010

Everyone Needs Help

Religion, to most, is considered to be the most important tool to have at your disposal when fighting the temptations that come your way in life. I have come to believe this to a certain extent. As opposed to me trying to force my particular belief system on you, I have chosen to address this topic under the guise of spirituality.

Many people have different names for God in terms of different genres, or denominations, but the underlying point is still correlated by one word, faith. Though I can respect it, I do not care what or who you call God in terms of names, I just think that it is important that you have a relationship with him. As a former atheist, it has taken me a long time to reach this conclusion, but it is one that I have come to on my own, so I know that it is coming from a sincere place.

We are all children of God, no matter who you are, whether you like it or not. He is the overall planner, the ultimate listener, the one who knows all and sets things in motion according to your choices. One common consensus amongst people in the streets is that if you turn to him after having made a mistake then you are not sincere. Another consensus amongst some people in society is that if you have a certain background, you don't belong with God, but rather someone else (Take a guess!). Neither of these notions are true, so they should not have an influence on your decision to try things according to another plan.

Some of God's most trusted and devoted followers were people who had made the same mistakes as us, no matter what you've done. You can read any holy book, and you will see him associating with people who have stolen, committed adultery, robbed, and what our society considers the ultimate no-no, murdered. Those who have made mistakes in life, are the best candidates to inspire change in others. Through people like us, God demonstrates that change is *always* possible. Society likes to put a time limit on it, if you don't do it before you land in a certain position then it's not real; or they will only attribute it to certain "types of people"; but he doesn't see it that way.

All that is required is sincerity, and commitment.

If you want a better way for yourself, and you are willing to do what is required according to what you believe, then he will help you. All you have to do is drop that heavy weight that is known as pride and ask for his help if you know the way, his guidance if you don't. This doesn't make you a chump or nothing of the sort. To the contrary, it shows an added level of courage because sometimes the hardest thing for people to do is to simply say "I don't know", or "Can you help me?".

Whether your mistakes have currently landed you in prison, or you are spiraling along a destructive path on the streets, you can still turn it around. It's not about you never being able to get out, or you not being viewed in the same light amongst your peers, it's about you wanting to be a better person. The brothers in this chapter have all viewed life through several optic lenses. I tried to diversify them to the best of my ability so that you could see that although they chose different faiths, they all arrived at the same place (so to speak), a place of true happiness. You can have that as well, a peace in your life that only comes as a direct result of peace of mind.

I hope that something that was said in this chapter, or this book, has inspired you to give God a try. You've been doing it your way up to this point, how do you honestly feel? If you are honestly not happy with your life right now, what do you have to lose? A little faith will take you a long way comrades, I give you my word on that.

In closing, I want to share some insightful words with you from the late, great Martin Luther King Jr.:

"Faith is taking the next step,
even when you can't see the entire staircase."

Closing Words From The Author

I started you off with my life and how it began in the beginning, but I neglected to share where I ended up with you, until now. My journey through the streets landed me on federal death row with not only a death sentence, but also consecutive life terms, as well as an additional fifty-five year sentence. Can you fathom that? The courts added all of that time on, even though they sentenced me to *die* first!

I have been incarcerated for almost twelve years to date, and I currently reside in a cell that only allows you to take five steps in one direction. There are one-hundred-and-sixty-eight hours in a single week. For me, one-hundred-and-sixty-two of those hours are spent inside of this cell. I am locked down almost all day, everyday. There is no reason for these people to let me out, I have a shower in here, I have to use the telephone in here, the television is in here, and they bring my food to me through a tray slot. My security level only allows me to have physical contact with up to five people at one time, and that is only possible after I have maintained a full year of what they call "clear" conduct. During the six hours that I am allowed out of my cell, I am taken outside to a cage (yeah, a cage) where I can exercise and get some "fresh" air. It's considered a privilege because out there you can take about fifteen steps in one direction before you walk into a metal fence.

This is no way to live young people, there isn't a single person here that thinks this is funny, or cool. I haven't seen my family since the day that I arrived here. Yeah I can talk to them, but a mother wants to see her child, a sister wants to hug her brother, a child wants to play with their dad. Even when my visiting day does come, none of these things will be possible because I can't even have contact with visitors.

I am not sharing these little details with you to garner sympathy, I just want you to see situations like this for exactly what they are. You now have the opportunity to see this place through my eyes, in an effort to either prevent you from taking this route, or prepare for your arrival. It's not about being tough, because I assure you that nobody is stab-proof or incapable of getting their ass whipped, by more than one person if need be. It's about being smart.

I remember growing up in the streets and seeing dudes come home from prison bigger, and sporting fresh tattoo's and thinking that was what prison was all about. An opportunity to become a better criminal. Not hardly. I have seen individuals who were tagged as being the toughest on the streets, get broken down in the prison environment. Guys who appeared heartless and cold, usually ended up having the most emotionally-gripping stories.

Stories that reveal hidden empathy, and human feelings, despite what others like to believe about us. Though these experiences vary from person to person, the point is that the lessons that came as a result of them were hard-earned.

I often sit around myself and add up all of the lessons that I had to pay way too much for. I hope that I accurately channeled some of my key experiences during each of the chapters in an effort to convey those very lessons. One of my biggest fears is that I may have missed something, something that may be key to opening your eyes and inspiring change. I put a tremendous amount of pressure on myself in the beginning to say all the "right" things in an effort to represent each individual that participated in this project in a positive light. It wasn't until I myself read each letter multiple times, that I came to the realization that such a thing was not possible. All I can do is give you the truth as I know it as an individual, so that you will at least have the opportunity to make an informed decision in your own lives. I am not perfect by a longshot, so please do not look at me, or any of these individuals that have shared their wisdom with you as so.

Another one of my fears, and perhaps my biggest, was simply putting my name as the author. I initially wanted to use a pseudonym, but after several conversations with people close to me, some of which participated in this project, I decided against it. In today's society, people tend to pay more attention to the messenger, rather than the message. I didn't want that for this book, or you. The fact that it was constructed from a hi-max security prison cell is completely irrelevant, when juxtaposed with it's intentions. I don't seek any recognition, or fame, from this. I just want it to get into as many hands as it can, so that hopefully an effective dialogue can get started and the young people can start to be understood and offered alternative solutions. This is my goal. I do not profess to be a "writer" or a genius that has the ability to change the world, but maybe I can reach a group of people who can. I am simply someone who got tired of hearing people praise prison life, and life in the streets, when they really have no clue what it's like. I got tired of people expecting destructive things to exit my mouth or manifest through my actions.

I made a conscious effort to work on my own life in all aspects. I used to be an avid user of curse words until one day I heard a single line that would spark the incentive to change that. That line was from the movie Malcolm X. In the movie Denzel Washington approached the character known as "Brother Baines" and commented on his self-control. He expressed the fact that he'd never heard him use profanity, and Brother Baines replied: "A man curses because he doesn't have the words to say what's on his mind." That single line caused me to look at myself in a different light on so many levels. Not only could I not carry a conversation without cursing, I could barely carry a conversation about anything other than street affairs. From that moment on, I decided to learn, and when I say learn, I mean everything. I studied words, history, myself, everything that I could until I started to notice a change not only in my thought patterns, but also my behavior. This led to me obtaining my G.E.D, and realizing that everything that I had taught myself, was exactly what I would have learned had I stayed in school as a kid. Subsequently, I found myself wondering if I would have ended up the same person had I acquired the knowledge that I now possessed earlier on.

Needless to say, that's neither here nor there now. I hadn't given myself a chance when it would have done me some good, and this is the result of that. My parents have had to watch me spiral out of control from the sidelines, my grandmother has had to endure tremendous emotional pain from her grandson, and I have to sit here and live with being the cause of all of this every single day until either I win my appeal, or I am executed. All of the people that were around me on the streets are either locked up, dead, or have found someone else to take my place. Out of all of the people that I knew, there are only about a handful of people that really cared, the majority of which are family.

So the next time you see someone who has just been released from prison and they appear to be a superstar in the eyes of the neighborhood, pull them to the side and ask them what it was really like underneath all of the glitz and glamour. If they are real, they will tell you that this is not what you want.

If you are a parent, talk to your kids about their future before it's too late and someone else does. Share some of your darkest secrets with them in an effort to boost your credibility. If they have dreams that you don't necessarily agree with, voice your concerns, but don't bash them. It's not your dream, it's their's. Establish yourself as a team, dedicated to helping them get to where they want to get to safely. Trust me, if you don't, someone else will, and the road in which they will take them to get there will be a little different.

In closing, to all of my critics. Yes, I am someone that has been tagged as a criminal and I wrote this book, get over it! Now can we please address the problems concerning our young people? If not, they have plenty of open cells here, and in other prisons all across the country, as well as graves to be filled for those who try to navigate their way through the world with no guidance.

Be Inspired!
K.J.L.